Live to Tell

Live to Tell

Evangelism in a
Postmodern World

Brad J. Kallenberg

Brazos Press
A Division of Baker Book House Co
Grand Rapids, Michigan 49516

Published by Brazos Press
a division of Baker Book House Company
P.O. Box 6287, Grand Rapids, MI 49516-6287

Printed in the United States of America

Library of Congress Cataloging-in-Publication Data

Kallenberg, Brad J.
    Live to tell : evangelism in a postmodern world / Brad J. Kallenberg.
        p.   cm.
    Includes bibliographical references.
    ISBN 1-58743-050-9 (pbk.)
    1. Evangelistic work. I. Title.
BV3790 .K25 2002
269′ .2—dc21   2002008657

For current information about all releases from Brazos Press, visit our web site:
http://www.brazospress.com

To Nancey Murphy,
a faithful mentor and loyal friend,
who never, never, never stopped
believing in me

Contents

Preface

Bruce was the most arrogant, self-centered jerk I had ever known. A loud-mouthed, inconsiderate upperclassman, he never thought twice about muscling a prepubescent twerp like me off of our school's gymnastic apparatus so he could show off to the passing girls. Then he would laugh like a buffoon. He disgusted me. *I*, on the other hand, was not like Bruce. I had been given a proper religious upbringing. I attended church five times per week. I had mastered hundreds of Bible verses and Protestant hymns. I—unlike Bruce—knew how to conduct myself with decorum and treat people with civility.

Two years passed and when I ran into Bruce again, this, this . . . *pagan* was leading the before-school student prayer meeting! Somewhere between junior high and high school he must have had a personality transplant. I heard him explain very simply that his life had been changed when he had begun a personal relationship with Jesus Christ. This caught me off guard. A personal relationship with Christ? I thought I had one of those.

Ironically, Bruce rapidly became my closest friend. His zest for life and joyful spirituality were infectious. I found myself spending as much time as I could with Bruce just to find out what made his faith so robust. He offered to share with me the not-so-secret ingredients that went into his recipe for joy. He showed me how God spoke to him through his Bible, which he studied for nearly two hours every day. He invited me to be a part of a small group of other believers that he was leading. He taught me how to play the guitar so we could "jam" together on Jesus People music. But above all, he introduced me to "sharing Christ" with others.

It was a Tuesday after school when I asked Bruce if he wanted to hang out together that evening. He declined, saying that he was doing something with Tom. Well, I knew Tom, so why didn't the three of us go out? Bruce explained mysteriously that he and Tom had "a standing appointment."

"An appointment—to do what?"

Bruce acted sheepish and coy—later I learned that he hadn't wanted to scare me off—but I finally wrung the truth out of him: every Tuesday Bruce and Tom met to pray, make phone calls, and witness. I got the uncanny feeling that my life was never going to be the same. They explained that they had been systematically calling through the hundreds of names in our high school directory, setting up times to meet classmates individually and tell them about Jesus. I excitedly begged them to let me tag along. I don't think they expected my enthusiasm. Warily they agreed.

At 8:00 we pulled up in front of Mark Somebody-or-Other's house. Bruce opted to pray while Tom and I approached the house. My enthusiasm for radical kingdom ministry felt more like raw fear. My mind raced. "The yard is fenced," I trembled, "that probably means dogs." Fortunately, man's best friend was nowhere in sight. As we climbed the porch steps I happened to glance in the window and saw—gasp—!—wine bottles on the kitchen counter. "Oh no, we're dealing with a family of alcoholics here!" We pushed the doorbell, and not one, but *three* hounds from hell charged through the kitchen. Someone answered the door. Frankly, I was feeling a little woozy and don't remember much of what happened next. After some confusion over why we were there to see a member of the household whom we had never met, Mark shuffled up from the basement and reluctantly endured our fifteen-minute exposé on Jesus, then got rid of us as quickly as he could.

As we headed back to the car, Tom was ruing the fact that Mark seemed entirely unmoved by the gospel, while I, I was strangely invigorated, as though someone had shot at me but missed. This was the most terrifying and rewarding thing I had ever done! I was hooked on evangelism.

For the next two years of high school and four years of college I had multiple conversations with people about Jesus every week. Riding the bus, sitting in the student union, eating pizza with dorm mates—I had an urgency to tell as many as I could about my Savior.

I took a bachelor of science degree in science education but entered a full-time career in evangelism. I spent what I consider the best decade of my life doing evangelism with university students in conjunction with a parachurch organization. What a great job—I was being *paid* to tell others the good news about Jesus! Eventually I pursued ordination, not as a pastor, but as an evangelist.

Of course, as I received training, my witnessing techniques became more sophisticated. I became interested in the sociology of conversion. Back in my high school days in the mid-seventies, one could pretty much count on 40 percent of college students being able to understand a gospel presentation simply by reading it. I came to learn, however, that by the mid-eighties only 20 percent could comprehend the gospel message. What was going on here?

Not only was the biblical literacy rate in decline, the conversion rate was slowly dropping as well. In the seventies, roughly 10 percent of our conversations with others about the gospel would culminate in conversion decisions. But by 1985, I was finding that I had to work twice as hard to fill a Bible study with new converts: the conversion rate seemed to hover around 6 or 7 percent. I was not overly concerned. After all, I had time to spare, and evangelism was my full-time job. But in the back of my mind was a nagging uneasiness: the window seemed to be closing.

Many ministries responded to the decreasing rate of conversion by borrowing mass-marketing techniques. We learned that radio spots, direct mailings, and newspaper ads could flush out those who were most interested in talking about Christ. Never mind any negative backlash; our morale was on the upswing. It was far more fun to contact people who had already expressed interest than to call randomly through a student directory. All that was needed was the money: for X dollars we could market to Y students, of whom Z would be eager to meet personally.

For a time, this approach breathed fresh life into an increasingly difficult occupation. On a campus the size of my alma mater, the 65,000-student University of Minnesota, the strategy kept the full-timers continuously busy. Unfortunately, the mass-marketing solution masked a deeper problem: the gospel was becoming a tough sell. A few years later I wasn't working at the "U," but was directing a team of nine full-timers and 100 student volunteers on a campus with only 6,000 students. By my calculations—gulp—the mass-marketing strategy was of no help at all: we would saturate the entire campus in September and glean only enough "hot contacts" to last through October!

That was 1989. Since then the conversion rate has continued to dwindle. I received a letter the other day from two colleagues who are faithfully serving Jesus in the area where I formerly worked. They reported that of the 213 students with whom they had conversations about Jesus this year, only four people became Christ-followers. You can do the math as well as I can—that's a conversion rate of less than 2 percent.

Granted, much of my data is anecdotal. But I strongly suspect that these stories could be endlessly multiplied. Those Willie Lomans who are now sweating as the window of opportunity closes in the West have doubled and tripled their efforts to salvage flagging ministries. On top of their exhaustion and discouragement is a false guilt; for what can one who is serving Jesus with a whole heart conclude in the face of such dismal statistics but that "I must be doing something wrong," or more dangerous, "Something must be wrong with me."

In 1989 I left campus ministry for graduate school in search of ways to cope with a culture that was changing under my feet.

In graduate school I learned that Western culture had taken a "postmodern" turn. What this amounts to is still very much up for grabs. But there doesn't seem to be much optimism that the West can ever turn back the clock. Is this regrettable? I'm not sure. It turns out that church history from the New Testament to the present shows that theology has always borrowed from philosophy to make its point with the regnant culture. In other words, it isn't just the "postmodern theologians" who are under the sway of philosophy. Theologians of the modern and premodern periods as well skillfully appropriated philosophy to do theology. Whether this was done explicitly (e.g., Aquinas's use of Aristotle) or implicitly (e.g., Augustine's use of Plato), such borrowing is always risky business, but a necessary one if we are to communicate the gospel. The only question that remains is whether we borrow wisely and with open eyes.

In such an age as ours, evangelism has become a cross-cultural task. We cannot take for granted any longer the common ground Christians once shared with Western culture. No longer is belief in God or the deity of Christ or the authority and inspiration of the Scriptures standard. In other words, we need to do as missionaries do: become students of the host culture so we can discover how God's Spirit intends the gospel to become embodied in the new era. Missiologists call this *contextualization*.[1]

Rather than gnash my teeth at the onrush of postmodernity, I wonder whether postmodern philosophy might provide a long awaited remedy to a Christianity grown somewhat ill through an overdose of modernity. After all, modernity has been no friend of the church. The medieval and Reformation periods could boast of nearly 100 percent church attendance among common folk, while modernity (from roughly 1650 on), for all its putative advantages, has seen church attendance plummet to a meager 3 percent throughout much of Europe.

I am not suggesting that postmodern philosophy is not without its own dangers. But I spent a long time studying that philosophy with the intent of understanding how we might "plunder the Egyptians." As it turns out, I think I have discovered many resources for recasting the way we do ministry in the contemporary culture.

What follows is my first attempt at expressing what it might mean to sing the gospel story in a postmodern key. I am grateful to Young Leaders Network for the chance to present this material at their regional forums in Baltimore, Minneapolis, and Dallas in 1999. The current form of the following essays owes much to my conversations with Christian ministers who attended the forums. I am particularly glad that pastors Brian McLaren, Doug Pagitt, Brad Cecil, Tony Jones, and Mark Miller shared with me stories of postmodern conversions that they had observed in their congregations. In addition, I am grateful for the insightful comments on an earlier draft of this work made by James William McClendon Jr., Nancey Murphy, Therese Lysaught, Stanley Hauerwas, Telford Work, Anne Collier-Freed, Christian Early, Ronnie Schwartz, and Allen Tennison. I also received perceptive comments from Meg Cox and the editorial team at Brazos Press led by Rodney Clapp. Thanks to all! Any remaining infelicities are, of course, my own.

1

Winds of Change
After Modernity

Rodney Clapp has recently identified Winnie-the-Pooh as a premier philosopher in the West. He writes:

> A noted Western philosopher, introduced to the world in 1926, was one day sitting on a log when he heard a buzzing sound. He was puzzled and fell to pondering. As his leading chronicler remembers the event, the philosopher reasoned along the following lines:
>
> "'If there's a buzzing-noise, somebody's making a buzzing noise, and the only reason for making a buzzing-noise that *I* know of is because you're a bee.'
>
> Then he thought another long time and said: 'And the only reason for being a bee that I know of is making honey.'

And then he got up and said: 'And the only reason for making honey is so *I* can eat it.'"[1]

Who can resist snickering at Pooh-bear's gleeful and unashamed preoccupation with his tummy? Yet, the reasoning process by which Pooh concludes that "bees are for *me*," epitomizes a widely accepted 300-year-old philosophical project. This project is the invisible backdrop to most of our contemporary preoccupations. Since the mid-seventeenth century, modern philosophy has advocated three doctrines.[2] First, the individual is always prior to and more significant than any larger group of which he or she is a part. According to this doctrine, sometimes called *generic individualism*, a believing community is incidental to, and really *nothing but*, the sum of the individual members. The real action takes place at the level of the individual who must choose his or her master, mate, and mission. Such decisions are taken to be the prerequisites for voluntary association with like-minded others.

A second modern doctrine holds that language is *nothing but* a picture of the world. Just as a Polaroid snapshot of my room does not rearrange the furniture, language is thought to be a neutral depiction of the way the world is. This reductive theory about language is called *representationalism*. According to representationalism, words and sentences are expendable bearers of more important things called meanings. In this view, truthfulness is measured in terms of a sentence's correspondence with the ways things really are.

It is claimed, third, that beliefs are *nothing but* assertions about the way things really are. This theory is sometimes called *propositionalism*. In this view, beliefs always can be, and ought to be, subject to rigorous testing. Those beliefs that pass the scrutiny of publicly accessible criteria qualify for the supreme status of "knowledge." However, strictly speaking, only in regard to logic and mathematics can the sentence "I *know*" be voiced truthfully—that is, with absolute certainty.

What could be more obvious?

Obvious for whom? Anything that strikes *Pooh* as obvious deserves a second look. Surprisingly, these three dogmas of modernity are themselves guilty of reductionism, the over simplification of complexities about selfhood, language, and faith.

These dogmas were not the achievement of millennia of searching after philosophical clarity. Rather, they were the emotional crutch of an age terrified by a world that was falling apart,[3] and recent philosophers have begun to migrate away from the conceptual space defined by these three doctrines of modernity.

Rather than spend time trying to make clear the modern views of metaphysics, language, or epistemology, by telling some stories I will try to give you some inkling of the sorts of directions in which contemporary postcritical or postmodern philosophy may be moving.[4] Once I clarify alternative ways for thinking about the world, I will make some suggestions as to what evangelism might look like in a post-Pooh age.

Challenging Individualism

According to the received account, conglomerates in the physical world are necessarily nothing more than the sums of their parts. For example, molecules are nothing more than the sum of their respective atoms; human persons are nothing more than the collection of their cells; communities are nothing more than the aggregation of their members, and so on.

On this old—and what we are calling here the modern—view, the *really real* and that which does all the causal work in any system are the smallest identifiable parts. Of course, this makes physics the premier scientific discipline because the direction of causation is assumed to move from parts to wholes, but not the other way around, and physics, after all, studies the smallest parts.

Yet if that were true, then we ought to be able predict the behavior of any group simply by looking at individuals. Unfortunately, this simply is not the case.[5] In fact, groups frequently take on a life of their own and act corporately as if the group were its own sort of entity. For example, imagine a herd of wild boars fleeing single-file through dense vegetation with a predator at their heels. Just as the predator is close enough to nibble the haunches of the last boar in the line something amazing happens. The pack splits, some running left, others running right, and as if on cue the entire herd turns to face the now-surrounded predator. How does each boar fleeing for its life manage to act in unison with the rest of the herd?

Or consider another puzzling story. The Hollywood hit *Jurassic Park* made famous the biological phenomenon that some species of African frogs have the ability to spontaneously change their gender in order to equilibrate a population in which one gender has disappeared. Let's say all the females have been removed. How is each male frog to know the difference between being continuously unlucky at getting a date for Saturday and the more serious condition (serious enough for him to change gender!) of there being no females at all in the community?

Consider a third example. We are all familiar with the ability of a school of fish to move in unified reaction to our tapping on the side of the aquarium. It might be hypothesized that unified movement is not a group behavior, but simply an accident: each individual fish is similar enough to the others to respond identically to the same external stimuli. If we managed to put tiny blindfolds on the fish and witnessed the same group behavior after tapping the glass, I suspect that we would be undaunted, for it is conceivable that the fish, each nearly identical to its neighbor, might be capable of responding to the sound or even to the vibration of our tapping. Of course this explanation only works if each fish possesses the faculty necessary for responding to sight, sound, or whatever. The real surprise would be if the school still swam in unison after, in addition to blindfolding them, we stopped their ears and scooped out their brains. And yet this is analogous to the Bénard phenomenon.[6] If a cylinder of liquid is heated from below, the blind, deaf, and witless molecules of the liquid spontaneously form hexagonal "cells" of convection as if an invisible honeycomb had been slipped into the container. Within each cell molecules move in a uniform way while molecules in a neighboring cell move in a different pattern that is uniform for that cell. How does any given molecule "know" to which cell it belongs?

What are we to make of these mysteries? Should we conclude that there *must* be a way to explain these group phenomena entirely in terms of the individuals because, after all, groups are *nothing but* the sum of their individual members? Some contemporary thinkers beg to differ; group behavior cannot be described in terms of individuals precisely because the group is *more than* the aggregation of its members. Something real emerges at the level of the group that has downward causal influence on the members. How else can we account for the behavior of the amoeba known as *Dictyostelium*?

> Normally, this single-celled organism goes about its quiet business of hunting down, engulfing and digesting bacteria that live in soil. After gorging itself sufficiently, *Dictyostelium* divides in two, and the new pair go their separate, bacteria-devouring ways. But if the thousands of *Dictyostelium* in a stamp-sized plot of soil should eat their surroundings clean, they do something exceptional. . . .
>
> Rather than crawling around randomly, the amoebas start streaming toward one another in inwardly pulsing ripples. As many as 100,000 converge in a swirling mound. And then, remarkably, the mound itself begins to act as if it were the organism. It stretches out into a bullet-shaped slug the size of a sand grain and begins to move. It slithers up toward the surface of the soil, probes specks of dirt, and turns around when it hits a dead end. Its movements are slow—it would need a day to travel an inch— but . . . the deliberateness of the movements eerily evoke an *it* rather than a *they*.[7]

Apparently, each *Dictyostelium* is able to take orders from the system of amoebas as a whole. To put it differently, the organisms form a group that attains something akin to group consciousness. Whatever the mechanism, the group appears able to influence its members by the transfer of information without which a given amoeba is unable to tell the difference between a localized food shortage and a regional famine. Notice that the direction of influence in this case is from the group to its members, or from the top down. This downward causation has an important correlate for human behavior.[8]

Imagine that you are the dean of students at a small Midwestern religious university and are leading an investigation into the suicide of a twenty-one-year-old white female student, Jane Doe. Relatives and acquaintances of all sorts have been interviewed for clues that might shed light on Jane Doe's choice to end her young life. The jigsaw puzzle of her life begins to take shape: the normally hard-working Jane had recently lost her job because she was unable to stay on task; her academic performance had suffered, with grades falling steadily over a six-month period; and a long-standing romantic relationship had soured, leaving Jane listless and depressed. And, oh yes, an autopsy showed that Jane had an unusually low ionic lithium concentration in her bloodstream—a condition typically associated with one form of manic depression.

Now, if asked to identify which of these was the *real* reason Jane committed suicide, the modern analyst would unhesitatingly point to the chemical deficiency as the root cause of Jane's behavior, on the assumption that Jane is *nothing but* the sum of her chemicals. But contemporary thinkers are unwilling to be so dismissive of what is a more complicated cluster of reasons each of which may have contributed to Jane's behavior. So, for example, one thinker might justifiably answer the question, "Why did Jane commit suicide?" by responding, "Because she was Protestant!"

How can this be? In 1897 Émile Durkheim, the father of sociology, published his finding that suicide rates vary according to victims' social groupings.[9] Protestants had higher suicide rates than Roman Catholics; city dwellers had a higher suicide incidence than their rural counterparts; and civilians were more likely to commit suicide than military personnel. Durkheim reasoned that groups displayed properties that individuals could not possess on their own. This is not unreasonable: a single H_2O molecule cannot display the property of wetness because more than one molecule is required to establish the surface tension considered characteristic of that we experience as wetness. Similarly, a single individual living in isolation cannot display the property of social cohesiveness. Durkheim hypothesized that groups vary according to levels of social cohesiveness. Some groups have a high degree of cohesion because members have internalized a strong normative framework closely tied with the group's identity—family obligations among Italians, religious duty among Roman Catholics, nationalist ideals among Shiite Muslims. Such normative frameworks possessed by the group and ingested by members make members resistant to suicide.

Durkheim's study of suicide is but one example of the way we are beginning to understand that groups achieve a certain level of reality. Properties emerge at the level of the group that can be neither reduced to those operating at the level of the individual nor completely explained only in terms of individuals. Moreover, the group as an ordered whole exerts a top-down influence on the individual members by virtue of these emergent group properties. Consequently, even the hardest of the sciences are, albeit reluctantly, beginning to admit that no one discipline has priority over the others; multiple levels of explanation are required because real causal influence emerges and operates at *all* levels of complexity.

Of course, it is relatively easy for us to admit that a chemical imbalance may cause aberrant behavior. But it takes much more to convince us that the reverse is also true: behavior alters brain chemistry.[10] In recent philosophical parlance, this more complicated picture of things is called *metaphysical holism:* a group may be *more than* the sum of its individual parts. In such cases, the group itself is causally real, influencing members from the top down.

Ironically, the notion of metaphysical holism is not a newfangled thing, but a very old concept that was lost sight of in the modern period. When the New Testament speaks of "the Body of Christ," the corporate filling of the Spirit, and the corporate "new man," or disapprovingly of "the Law"[11] and "principalities and powers,"[12] it is acknowledging powers that are inextricably bound up with community life and that hold sway over the individual.[13] To anticipate a topic I will take up in more detail later, we can at least provisionally conclude that faithfulness in evangelism must simultaneously attend to both the group and the individual. But before we consider evangelism, we must consider two other ways modernity is becoming antiquated.

Language Constitutes the World

A second way in which contemporary thinking is leaving the conceptual space of modernity is by acknowledging the way that language constitutes the world.

The urgency modern thinkers feel for doing analysis misleads them: they try to understand the mechanism of language by misconstruing language as one thing and the world as another, and then investigating the relationship between the two. The nearly unanimous conclusion of this approach has been that language simply pictures the world.

This strategy is flawed from the outset. What does it mean to treat language in isolation from the world and the world in isolation from language when we think *by means of* language? I cannot treat the world in isolation from language because it is by means of language that I treat anything at all.

Consider: it is tempting to assume that the mind operates like some sort of digital camera that stores a staggering number of freeze-frame snapshots as we proceed through a day. Such snapshots are thought to be, in principle at least, available for recall and review by the adequately trained brain. A verbal description of the image is thought to be a secondary, add-on step in the processing of sensory data. However, as Ludwig Wittgenstein observed, an astonishingly high percentage of our mental life cannot be accomplished merely by sequences of images. For example, try thinking *I expect it to stop raining soon* without using words. We can conjure images of it raining and then not raining. But what would an image of "expectation" or "soonness" look like? That an expectation can be about an imminent state of affairs that may or may not come to pass (it may rain for another week!) is central to the meaning of this sentence. As it turns out, words such as "expect" and "soon" are not incidental add-ons to fundamentally image-based mental processing. Rather, we cannot catch the principle drift of the sentence without using these very words because *language is the means by which we think*.[14]

We can also get an inkling that the modern approach may be deeply flawed by noting that if language were merely a picture, it could be learned by pointing and naming. However, Wittgenstein showed that a word can be defined by pointing to something only when the overall role of the word in the language is already clear.[15]

Suppose, however, someone were to object: "It is not true that you must already be master of a language in order to understand an ostensive definition: all you need—of course!—is to know or guess what the person giving the explanation is pointing to. That is, whether for example to the shape of the object, or to its color, or to its number, and so on."

Wittgenstein answers his imaginary interlocutor: "And what does 'pointing to the shape', 'pointing to the color' consist in? Point to a piece of paper.—And now point to its shape—now to its color—now to its number (that sounds queer).—How did you do it?"[16] Because the same gesture in each instance is intended to pick out vastly different aspects (shape, color, number, and so on), pointing cannot be the basis by which a nonspeaker acquires fluency in language, especially his or her first language.

One of my earliest memories is of an event that occurred when I was too young to have mastered the names of the primary colors. I recall my friends teasing me for not knowing my colors. I must have insisted otherwise because one of them chirped, "Oh yeah, then what is this?" while pointing on a page in a coloring book. "That," she cried triumphantly, "is yellow!" I went home very confused because I knew she had pointed to a pear. I could not understand her gesture of pointing until I understood how to use the words *color* and, in particular, *yellow* in English sentences.

Children initially learn a language not by having objects pointed out to them—that game comes very much later—but by being trained into a form of life. All of us share primitive reactions—we squint at bright lights, we pucker when we suck lemons, and so on. Wittgenstein calls these behaviors primitive reactions in order to emphasize their givenness for the functioning of language. One way (and only one way) to think of the connection between primitive reactions and language use is to imagine language as going proxy for these other behaviors.

> How do words *refer* to sensations? . . . Here is one possibility: words are connected with the primitive, the natural, expressions of the sensation and used in their place. A child has hurt himself and he cries; and then adults talk to him and teach him exclamations and, later, sentences. They teach the child new pain-behavior.
>
> "So you are saying that the word 'pain' really means crying?"— On the contrary: the verbal expression of pain replaces crying and does not describe it.[17]

Wittgenstein's point is that language doesn't *refer to*, or *picture*, or *correspond to*, or *depict* some nonlinguistic reality; there

23

is no way for us to imagine that to which language corresponds ("a state of affairs," "the world," "reality," etc.) except in terms of the very language that this "reality" is supposed to be considered in isolation from. Rather, learning a language is an irreducibly social enterprise that trains a child into a communal mode of living.[18] Thus Wittgenstein likens language to a series of games that require partners for playing: "In a conversation: One person throws a ball; the other does not know: whether he is supposed to throw it back, or throw it to a third person, or leave it on the ground, or pick it up and put it in his pocket, etc."[19] Language is not a picture that succumbs to distanced observation, it is a socially involved enterprise that by its very nature engages human subjects.

We now can see why another radical critic of modernity, John L. Austin, describes language as "performative."[20] Language is a form of action that gets work done. Think of the vast array of ways in which language performs work: we make promises, we ask questions, we give orders, we make confessions. When I spoke the words "I do!" to Jeanne L. Dahle, I didn't describe some state of affairs—I changed forever both her world and mine. With and through those words I became her husband. More ominously, now that we have children, we are painfully aware of the power of language to nurture or denature our three children, who inhabit a world of either praise or verbal abuse.

Thus, philosophy has challenged some long-standing assumptions about language. Before I show these recent views' significance for doing ministry, let me introduce one more way contemporary thinking is leaving modernity behind.

The Shifting of Paradigms

Nicolaus Copernicus was a Polish astronomer whose posthumous publication with the snappy title *On the Revolution of the Celestial Orbs* (1543) turned the world on its head. Copernicus used geometry to argue that, contrary to common thinking, the Earth revolved around the sun in a regular orbit. By 1610 Galileo Galilei had begun publishing observations of the heavens that he had made by means of his telescope. These observations corroborated Copernicus's heliocentric model. Despite violent opposition from the church, multitudes of thinking people were converted to the view that we inhabit a solar system, with the sun at its center, rather than a geocentric, or Earth-centered, universe.

We must understand that the stakes for such a conversion were high. Astronomy was not simply a hobby for those who had the money and leisure to gaze heavenward. Charting the stars was critical for navigating Earth's oceans, and knowledge of the heavenly seasons was integral to skillfully timing the planting and harvesting of crops. And for thousands of years, the Earth-centered model of the Egyptian astronomer Ptolemy had generated exceptionally accurate star charts and calendars. To give up this system surely could be done rationally only on the basis of improved charts and calendars. Right? Wrong! The real puzzle surrounding the mass conversion to the Copernican view was the fact that empirical data, such as those improved charts and calendars, lagged behind the Ptolemaic system by nearly two hundred years![21] We normally say that when we change our minds, we did so on the basis of solid evidence. How can we account for this mystery?

In 1951 W. V. O. Quine shocked the philosophical world with the suggestion that beliefs are as social as they are rational.

> The totality of our so-called knowledge or beliefs, from the most casual matters of geography and history to the profoundest laws of atomic physics or even of pure mathematics and logic, is a man-made fabric which impinges on experience only along the edges. . . . But the total field is so undetermined by its boundary conditions, experience, that there is much latitude of choice as to what statements to re-evaluate in the light of any single contrary experience. No particular experiences are linked with any particular statements in the interior of the field, except indirectly through considerations of equilibrium affecting the field as a whole.[22]

Quine suggested that we understand human beliefs as the shared property of a human community.[23] Beliefs form an interlocking set; each belief has a stake in the reliability of neighboring beliefs. Experience impinges only on the set as a whole by being the "boundary condition" of the web. Experience may indeed conflict with beliefs, but in such cases, the conflict is not between an isolated belief and a single datum of experience. Rather, experience as a whole may generate dissonance within the entire web. As tension mounts, the community rushes to reestablish equilibrium by a variety of strategies.

To put it differently, beliefs differ from each other only by virtue of their distance from the periphery of experience. Those beliefs that lie near the periphery are more public and more open to change. Those beliefs that are more deeply ingressed are more impervious to change. One can imagine that central beliefs are hedged in by a buffer of more peripheral beliefs. Tension may be resolved by one of three strategies, any of which may be reasonable.

First, the recalcitrant data may simply be ignored. Scientists regularly suspend final judgment on puzzling experiment results when these results seem to undermine reigning scientific views. For example, scattered reports of experiments in which nuclear fusion is achieved at room temperature will continue to be treated with suspicion precisely because the possibility of cold fusion runs against the grain of contemporary theoretical physics. Two facts make the current web of beliefs very resilient to change: first, too much has been invested (time, research dollars, textbook production, etc.) to scrap it all on the basis of one or two anomalies; second, the reigning web of beliefs has a vastly greater success rate at explaining hundreds of thousands of experimental data than any yet-to-be-formulated replacement created to account for the single puzzling anomaly. Thus, one reasonable response is to adopt a wait-and-see attitude in anticipation that some fertile minds may eventually concoct ways to understand present anomalies within the spectrum of currently available theories. And, as the history of science bears out, in most cases such a resolution presents itself.

Second, sometimes tension may be resolved by inventing a belief that mollifies the tension by realigning the web. Consider a theological example. Early Christians clearly believed that (1) Jesus was to be worshiped as God, (2) God was one, and (3) Jesus and God were distinct. It didn't take long for detractors to object that these beliefs constituted a logical contradiction. Of course, the problem would dissolve if Christians were willing simply to jettison one of these three beliefs, but too much was at stake. Denial of Christ's deity is the subordinationist heresy practiced by the Arians. Denial of the unity of God would be tantamount to polytheism (or literally, bi- or tritheism). Denial of the distinction between Jesus and the Father winds up in the heresy called modalism. In order to retain all three beliefs, Christians constructed the doctrine of the Trinity, which relieved the tension. The deity of Christ, the singularity of God, and the distinctiveness of the Father and the Son were each intelligible when viewed under the concept aspect of the Trinity.

Does this mean that the Trinity is just a fiction because it was an invention of the believing community? This question is wrongheaded. Let me illustrate with an example from the world of engineering. Bridges are always in danger of collapsing because winds and traffic set them vibrating like guitar strings. If the vibrations resonate—a phenomenon in which the amplitude, or strength, of the vibration surges because it matches the natural wavelength of the span of the bridge—the bridge is in danger of collapsing. To avoid catastrophe, bridge designers must estimate this danger by solving what are called wave equations for the bridge. If the solution to the wave equation turns out to be a certain imaginary number (such as $\sqrt{-1}$), the bridge will not collapse from vibrational stresses. Yet imaginary numbers are so called because they cannot be located anywhere on the real number line. Does this make them simply fictitious? Of course not. Imaginary numbers are real in the sense that they are shorthand accounts of safe bridges. Similarly, the concept of the Trinity is a shorthand reminder of safe ways we need to travel when speaking about God. To speak about God in any other way will land us in heresy.

Third, tension in the web resulting from the web's inability to reconcile itself to recalcitrant experience may eventually tear the fabric of the web. When this sort of crisis occurs, a large set or subset of beliefs may be supplanted by another set altogether. This wholesale exchange of belief systems is called a *paradigm shift*. Because swapping takes place in blockhouse fashion, there is not usually a smooth transition from one paradigm to another. Rather, the transition is like a Gestalt switch. For example, most Westerners instinctively see the following figure in one of two ways: as a three dimensional box coming toward and down to the left of the viewer or as one coming toward them but up to the right. Once a viewer fixates on one of these aspects, she can force herself to see it under the other aspect. However, when this change of aspect dawns, it happens all at once; the figure doesn't morph from one aspect to the other—it *leaps*.

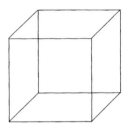

Similarly, when a paradigm is in crisis, the shift to a new paradigm is very rapid and has naturally been described as "a conversion."[24] However, unlike a Gestalt switch, a paradigm shift generally is not reversible; once the new paradigm is in place, the old way of viewing things is no longer convincing.

On the other hand, because data gain significance only by virtue of their appropriation and interpretation by a conceptual scheme (a paradigm is the means by which we interpret data *as data*),[25] the shifting of paradigms cannot be driven by data alone. Thomas Kuhn explains:

> The man who embraces a new paradigm at an early stage must often do so in defiance of the evidence provided by problem-solving. He must, that is, have faith that the new paradigm will succeed with the many large problems that confront it, knowing only that the older paradigm has failed with a few. A decision of that kind can only be made on faith.[26]

Thus, the swapping of paradigms is reasonable—we have epistemic permission to shop around once our old paradigm is in crisis—but it is never, strictly speaking, *compelled* by the data for which the new paradigm provides a radically different (incommensurable) interpretation.[27] We can now appreciate the ambiguity facing early admirers of Copernicus. Copernicus's geometry seemed to make sense, but Ptolemy's model produced (at that time) more accurate calendars. So, what was one to do? In Kuhn's words, those who converted to the Copernican model did so on the basis of faith.

Summary

By and large, the differences between the received modernist account of reality and that offered by recent postmodern upstarts are so great that it is natural for postmodern (or postcritical) thinkers to speak of their own work as constituting a paradigm shift. I have discussed three aspects of this new paradigm in particular. First, *metaphysical holism* is the view that groups behave like real entities that both constitute each member's identity and have top-down causal influence on them. Hence, we are socially constituted critters. Second, language accounts for the lion's share of our social make-up (*linguistic holism*); language is the means by which we think and act in the world. Language cannot be pried off the world of experience and analyzed in isolation because the conceptual language we think and speak determines the shape of the world we inhabit. Third, the beliefs we hold about our world form an interlocking set that we share with the rest of our community (*epistemological holism*). This set of beliefs, or paradigm, is very resilient and typically resists change. But when change comes, it comes all at once.

Although these new habits of speaking cannot be easily explained (especially in terms of the modern paradigm), they have direct implications for understanding evangelism and religious conversion. Let's tackle conversion first.

2

A Fresh Look
at Conversion

When a person comes to Christ, such a one "becomes a new person altogether—the past is finished and gone, everything has become fresh and new!" This miracle can only be ascribed to God: "All this is God's doing, for he has reconciled us to himself through Jesus Christ" (2 Cor. 5:17–18 PHILLIPS). Viewed from the side of God, nothing more needs to be said. No human assistance is needed. No one earns salvation; no one contributes in any way to the gift that comes to us from God entirely by means of grace.

Yet, the phenomenon of conversion can also be described from the human side.[1] Behaviors change, associations change, directions change. In fact, the term *conversion* very simply means "change." Jesus himself affirmed that change corroborated conversion, for "each tree is known by its own fruit" (Luke 6:43–45 NRSV).

In viewing conversion from the human side, we might ask how it can be described in postmodern terms. Simply put, when viewed through a postcritical lens, conversion can be understood as entailing the change of one's social identity, the acquisition of a new conceptual language, and the shifting of one's paradigm.[2]

Conversion as a Change of Social Identity

When we are asked to identify something, we generally take one of two approaches. The first approach is analysis. Imagine that someone offers to sell you a Rolex watch for five dollars. Now even a broken Rolex is worth more than five dollars; if the watch is repaired it might be sold for many times that amount. Then it dawns on you—perhaps there are no insides to this particular Rolex. How can you correctly distinguish a broken Rolex from an empty Rolex casing? Easy—take it apart. This strategy is called analysis. What we assume to be the critical identifiers of an object are thought to lie within the object and must be brought to light by disassembling it.

Consider a second scenario. You walk out to your friend's garage. Standing there, you are intrigued by what appear to be random piles of metal scraps. Approaching one pile, you ask yourself, "What is this?" With a little skill, a lot of patience, and even more luck you manage to assemble the first pile into a mechanism of some sort. Although you feel reasonably sure that you've assembled it correctly, you still may not be able to identify it. Clearly, taking it apart again will not solve the puzzle because you did not know what it was before you began. Operating under the assumption that all the piles form a coherent whole, you decide that the mystery of the mechanism you've assembled will be solved only when you've finished assembling all of the piles. As it turns out, the machine is a motorcycle and the mechanism its carburetor.

This second strategy for identifying an object moves in a direction opposite of the first. While analysis identifies an object by disassembling it and labeling its constitutive parts, holism identifies an object by understanding its function in a larger scheme. This larger context is not incidental to the object; rather, a complete description of the object *necessarily* includes description of the context. The object is what it is precisely because of its context.

Imagine a friend remarking on a Rembrandt painting, "I am quite taken by the color of this character's eye. I think I'll paint my house just this color." So they take a print of the Rembrandt down to the hardware store with the nifty computerized color-match spectrometer, and return home with 10 gallons of special mix house paint. Bad plan! Its tough enough to pick a house color by looking at "painter-approved" colors on two-by-two swatches. Just ask the folks who live on Eighth Avenue in Houghton, Michigan. They will simply shake their heads and point ruefully to 1105: "See that house? Kallenbergs painted it in 1987." Although we had done our best to pick a pleasing paint chip, once we got it on the house it looked like an entirely different color. We thought the paint store had mixed us the wrong color. But when we held up the paint chip, it was a dead match. So why did it look so bad on the house? The paint chip held in our hand, like the color of the eye in the Rembrandt painting, had an entirely different context than the paint on the exterior walls of a house surrounded by lawn and trees and sky. The context made each color what it was.

In this vein, Wittgenstein once suggested that changing the context all but physically transforms an object into something quite different:

> Look at a long-familiar piece of furniture in its old place in your room. You would like to say: "It is part of an organism." I could give this thing a name and say that it . . . has a stain, is dusty; but if I tried taking it *quite* out of its present context, I should say that it had ceased to exist and another had gotten into its place.
>
> One might feel like this: "Everything is part and parcel of everything else" (internal and external relations). Displace a piece and it is no longer what it was. Only in this surrounding is this table this table. Everything is part of everything.[3]

The fact that Wittgenstein's comments sound odd to us may be symptomatic of the way that we in the modern West, for whatever reason, have become accustomed to the analytical strategy for identification while our skill for seeing connections has atrophied. And yet we can profitably ask: "Which strategy is more helpful for understanding human identity?"

When we are asked to identify ourselves, we quite naturally tell stories. When Lars states that he is a Norwegian bachelor farmer, he is offering a shorthand version of longer stories he could tell that situate him within his social world. Each story contributes to his identity, makes him who he is, by virtue of his relationships with others, relationships that together constitute the warp and weft of his identity just as he is a strand in the fabric of theirs.

Alasdair MacIntyre suggests that our penchant for telling stories is a clue to the irreducibly narrative fabric of our existence. In other words, any account of the human person that leaves out narrative is grossly reductionistic. MacIntyre invites us to live the following scenario with him.

> I am standing waiting for a bus and the young man standing next to me suddenly says: "The name of the common wild duck is *Histrionicus histrionicus histrionicus*." There is no problem as to the meaning of the sentence he uttered: the problem is, how to answer the question, what was he doing uttering it? Suppose he just uttered such sentences at random intervals; this would be one possible form of madness. We would render his action of utterance intelligible if one of the following turned out to be true. He has mistaken me for someone who yesterday had approached him in the library and asked: "Do you by chance know the Latin name of the common wild duck?" *Or* he has just come from a session with his psychotherapist who has urged him to break down his shyness by talking to strangers. "But what shall I say?" "Oh, anything at all." *Or* he is a Soviet spy waiting at a prearranged rendez-vous and uttering the ill-chosen code sentence which will identify him to his contact. In each case the act of utterance becomes intelligible by finding its place in a narrative.[4]

What is MacIntyre's point? We can understand the meaning of the young man's sentence by a using simple process of analysis. We easily identify the subject ("The name of the common wild duck"), the copulative verb ("is"), and the nominative predicate (the Latin term, *"Histrionicus histrionicus histrionicus"*).

But analysis only gets us so far. We cannot understand the significance of the sentence without discovering more about the context in which it was spoken. In other words, in order for this sentence to be fully intelligible, it must also be understood holistically, and not merely analytically. In short, we need the rest of the story.

Of course, the mystery sentence is itself an action taken by a human being. As it turns out, every human action (not just sentences) become fully intelligible only when seen in the context of a string of actions, and strings of actions interweave to convey an episode. A long sequence of episodes tell the story of a single human life, a biography, and each human life is ultimately intelligible only when understood as a thread in a much more tangled skein—communal history, human history, the history of the cosmos, and perhaps even the story of God. Only to the extent that an event is seen against the backdrop of this greater weave of context can its full significance be grasped.

MacIntyre's insight taps deeply into ancient wisdom. Premodern, as well as non-Western, thinkers utilize a holistic strategy—a narrative rather than an analytical one—quite naturally when answering the question "Who am I?"[5] Consider St. Augustine's religious conversion as recorded in his autobiography known as *The Confessions*.[6]

Augustine was born on November 13, 354, in Thagaste near the eastern border of present-day Algeria. Augustine's father, Patricius, a property owner and town councilor, was wealthy enough for Augustine to study pagan literature in nearby Madauros at age eleven but not wealthy enough for him to continue his education past age fifteen. Augustine returned to Thagaste and idled away his sixteenth year. The following year a wealthy citizen of Thagaste sponsored Augustine's education. He enrolled in rhetorical school in Carthage, and in the same year his father died. By the time Augustine was eighteen he had taken a mistress and fathered a child out of wedlock. While in Carthage he also became an auditor of the Manichaeans, a pseudo-Christian sect. During the nine years he studied Manichaeanism, Augustine established several oratory schools and eventually became a professor of rhetoric in Milan. After abandoning Manichaeanism he dabbled in Neoplatonic philosophy and at the same time became impressed with the rhetorical skill of a Christian preacher named

Ambrose. Intrigued by Ambrose's style, he was captured by Ambrose's gospel and became a catechumen of the church. Three years later (A.D. 386) he resigned his chair in rhetoric and converted to Christianity. He was baptized the following Easter at the age of thirty-three.

Several events stand out in Augustine's memory. He vividly recalls the licentious and rowdy character of his sixteenth year, epitomized by the theft of some pears from a neighbor's tree. What horrified Augustine was not the magnitude of this sin, but its wanton character. To steal fruit when one did not need to—after tasting the pears, the gang of adolescents threw them to the pigs—was to steal it simply for the pleasure of doing what was forbidden.[7]

In general terms, the most striking characteristic of Augustine's memory of preconversion events is its disjointed character. From a distance his life looks like this: reads pagan literature in Madauros; idles away a year in Thagaste; studies rhetoric in Carthage; takes a mistress; fathers a child; teaches rhetoric; joins a cult; moves to Italy; studies philosophy; converts to Christianity. Because of the random and disjointed character of this list, it is tempting to wonder whether the last item is just one more passing phase, namely that of "getting religion." Might not such a phase be expected to soon pass? So why did this last "phase" stick? There are two reasons.

First, Augustine abandoned Manichaeanism not simply because of the content of its teachings but also because of the *form* of its teachings. By the fourth century, Manichaeans had developed a highly theoretical mode of philosophical explanation. The goal of this enterprise was to tackle difficult questions—for example, Why does evil exist?—by explaining away the enigma in light of an all-encompassing theoretical system. Augustine rightly suspected that evil was evil precisely because of its pointless character (remember the pears). To *explain* evil would therefore give evil a reason, a result that runs against the grain of its basic pointlessness. Moreover, a philosophical scheme that explains absolutely everything forces one to misconstrue even God as knuckling under to the system. Not only does an explanatory mode of philosophy wind up limiting God's freedom, and hence God's agency or personalness, but also the success of any explanation of evil undermines the human need to repent; the more totalizing the explanatory scheme, the less I am responsible for my actions.

Thus Augustine's first moment of conversion was his abandonment of the very theoretical mode of reasoning that made Manichaeanism a philosophical system.[8] We can see why this move might make sense: divine revelation comes to us in the form of a story because God's dealings with us are narratively shaped rather than theoretically driven. In other words, God sent us a gospel rather than a philosophical treatise! Therefore, step one for Augustine came in the form of a realization that he needed not a system or a theory, but a story. Then the important question became: Which story is true? Of course, Augustine could not revert to a theoretical analysis of truth or of theories of truth without backsliding into the very mode of reasoning he had just abandoned. Rather, he learned that the verdict "This story is true" is a *self*-involving judgment.

The second moment in Augustine's conversion was his embrace of the gospel as the truth. As Stanley Hauerwas and David Burrell summarize, "The narrative Augustine tells [in *Confessions*] shows how he was moved to accept the gospel story by allowing it to shape his own."[9] To say the same thing differently, I cannot judge or confess that a story that involves me is true unless the story shapes my life. To call a story true is to trust it to be a reliable guide for interpreting my past and navigating my future. What Augustine discovered was the gospel's power to knit together the disjointed phases of his life in such a way that he could perceive them as episodes in a story, much older than his own, of a restless quest for God. The gospel could not be regarded by Augustine as true and also be simply a passing phase. Before his conversion, Augustine admitted, his life was so random and chaotic that he had no self to speak of. But after God "shattered his deafness" and "drove away his blindness," Augustine discovered his true self through the lens of the gospel: all of the fads that characterized his early life were now seen as episodes in the single story of a life questing for God.[10] He summarized this quest in the opening pages of *Confessions*: "for you have made us for yourself, and our heart is restless until it rests in you."[11]

In deeming the gospel true, Augustine was not only allowing the story of God to make sense of his past, he was also allowing it to shape his future by joining its story line. In other words, to be a Christ-follower is to become a character who contributes to the continual telling, retelling, and re-retelling of Christ's story. At bottom, any story that does not have the power to reproduce the qualities of its protagonist in the life of the readers should be discarded as trivial.

Unfortunately, there are powerful, enduring, dark stories that rival the gospel. Nietzsche's tale of *Übermensch* was reproduced in Hitler's life. However, both sorts of stories, of darkness and of light, are forms of rebellion against the gray twilight of modernity, which falsely assures its citizens that stories are merely ornamental to authentic human living. On the contrary, the battle for human souls is a war fought with the weapons of stories. [12]

Augustine's conviction of the gospel's truthfulness was not a theoretical exercise of piling proposition upon proposition until finally a conclusion was entailed. Rather, Augustine underwent a conversion: he was graced with a new story and thus a new self that came to him by means of the gospel which simultaneously revealed to him who he was and whose he was.

Recent trends in postcritical philosophy, then, suggest one way in which we can more richly understand the human side of conversion, namely, as the acquisition of a new identity. This identity is not revealed by analyzing oneself into one's constituent parts but by understanding one's place in the story line of the gospel. This story line does not end with the resurrection of Christ or with the expansion of the church from Jerusalem to Rome. Rather it continues in the telling and retelling of the gospel to all the nations. Only when this has been completed can the end be written (Matt. 24:14). Because this story line is lived out by the community of Christ-followers, the new convert's identity is necessarily social; one cannot identify oneself as a Christ-follower and avoid identifying oneself with the believing community that is seeking to embody the gospel both in its words and in its life together.

Conversion as Acquisition of a New Conceptual Language

A second resource for enriching our understanding of conversion runs parallel to the second way postcritical thinking transcends modern views of language. Put simply, conversion involves the acquisition of a new conceptual language.

Scientist-cum-linguist Benjamin Whorf made the observation that in order to understand the world we must already be skilled in a language because we use language to think.[13] He opens the title essay of his book *Language, Thought, and Reality* with words from Edward Sapir:

> Human beings do not live in the objective world alone, not alone in the world of social activity as ordinarily understood, but are very much at the mercy of the particular language which has become the medium of expression for their society. It is quite an illusion to imagine that one adjusts to reality essentially without the use of communication or reflection. The fact of the matter is that the "real world" is to a large extent unconsciously built up on the language habits of the group. . . . We see and hear and otherwise experience very largely as we do because the language habits of our community predispose certain choices of interpretations.[14]

The character of one's experience is internally related to the character of one's conceptual language. These are two sides of the same coin. For example, we in the West naturally divvy up the world into objects and events because Indo-European languages communicate predominately by means of two classes of words: nouns (corresponding to objects) and verbs (corresponding to events). In contrast, Nootka, a language native to Vancouver Island, has no nouns. "A house occurs" or "it houses" (perhaps analogous to the way we say "a flame burns" or "it flames") is the Nootka equivalent of saying "house." Similarly, Whorf notes that the language of the Hopi Indians might be considered a "timeless language." The notions of simultaneity and of treating time as an object ("time marched on") cannot be conveyed in Hopi. Nor is it possible to express the passing of time with a plural noun; one might say "I left on the fifth day," but never "I stayed five days."

The difference between our language and that of Hopi (or Nootka) is so great that we may be tempted to disbelieve what linguists tell us is true. "Surely," we might oject, "there *must* be a way for the Hopi to *count* time. If not, they can't even do basic physics." One can see how easily prejudice grows in the soil of difference. In fact the Hopi do get along in the world as well as English speakers do. And I suspect that a physics textbook could be written in the Hopi language. My point is simply this: any physics text written in the Hopi language would be vastly different from ours because the concepts the language has to work with are vastly different from those of our language.

We can understand the way language shapes each person's world when we imagine the way a child learns a language.

> The content of what is said by toddlers is very much the same whether they speak a primitive or a modern tongue. In both cases they express the same elementary needs and reactions in basically the same worlds of objects to be enjoyed or avoided and of persons to be trusted or feared. But one language may in the long run open up all the riches of human history and of a vastly promising though ominous future, while the other, the better a child learns it, imprisons him more tightly in his little tribe or village. At two years of age, the member of a preliterate culture might still be a potential Confucius, Newton, or Beethoven; at twenty, never.[15]

With these words George Lindbeck is claiming that the learning of language leaves a permanent mark on the growing child. We know in some cases that this is physically true: adults who learn a second language have much more difficulty shedding their accents than do children who become bilingual. (Although my high school biology teacher had taught in the Scandinavian Midwest states, he was never able to say "Ya hey, you bet'cha" without a thick Slavic accent.) Just as the speaking of a language leaves a lasting imprint on a child's facial and vocal muscles, the thinking with a language leaves a lasting imprint on the growing child's mind.

Lindbeck goes on to suggest that one's *religious* world is likewise limited or expanded by the conceptual language one has at one's disposal since "it is necessary to have the means for expressing an experience in order to have it." He concludes, "the richer our expressive or linguistic system, the more subtle, varied, and differentiated can be our experience."[16] One of the benefits of theological education is precisely the expansion of nuance in discernment of religious experience that comes with the expansion of one's theological vocabulary. But at a more basic level, Lindbeck is implying that there are no analogs for notions such as "sin" or "answers to prayer" in the secular conceptual language. The only way one can conceive human depravity correctly is by being schooled in the use of the term *sin* within sentences spoken in the Christian language. And only those who are fluent in the use of terms and phrases such as *grace* and *answers to prayer* can see a set of circumstances as an answer to prayer rather than as a remarkable coincidence. If Lindbeck is correct about the significant role language plays in enabling religious experience, then it follows that religious conversion necessarily includes the acquisition of the appropriate conceptual language.[17]

There are at least two important facets of this process of language learning. On the one hand, fluency is gained by participation in the linguistic community's *form of life*—that weave of activity, relationships, and speech that gives the community its unique personality. For example, Wittgenstein carefully remarked that "It is part of the grammar of the word 'chair' that *this* [sitting down] is what we call 'to sit on a chair.'"[18] His point? We only truly understand how to use the word *chair* in a sentence by virtue of our contact with chairs. Chairs are things we sit in, fetch, count, reupholster, stand on, trip over, stub our toes on, and so on. Without these activities, "chair" would be a vacuous concept. Now think of how a child learns to correctly use the term *God*. For a child, "God" is neither "the ground of our Being" nor "the first cause," but "the one we pray to . . . and thank before we eat . . . and sing songs about . . . and tell our friends about . . . and confess our sins to." Only by virtue of these activities does the word *God* come to mean anything at all. In this light, the atheist, who neither prays to, thanks, sings to, witnesses about, or confesses to God, may be correct to deny the existence of "God" because what the atheist means by the word *God* is an empty concept!

A second way that we learn a conceptual language is by means of our community's stockpile of interpretive stories. When my son Daniel was ten years old, he asked why I wouldn't allow him to watch the Sylvester Stallone blockbuster movie *Cliffhanger*. I explained that not only may watching violence harden one's heart, but also if the hero uses sinful means, albeit to accomplish righteous ends, then to cheer for the hero is to cheer for the wrong team. Moreover, watching violence may make us into people of violence. "If all the gang members lived on farms and learned to work hard instead of watching violent TV and movies, don't you think that crime would drop?" Danny's instantaneous reply was telling: "Oh, you mean like in the movie, *Dark Horse*?" Whether or not you agree with the points I made about violence, can you see what just happened? Danny used a movie he had seen to understand the moral lesson I was trying to teach him. Just as maps help us navigate our physical terrain, stories provide us with clues and role models for helping us comprehend and achieve our proper ends. As Alasdair MacIntyre has poignantly noted, "Deprive children of stories and you leave them unscripted, anxious stutterers in their actions as in their words."[19]

To sum, conversion, when understood from the human side and in terms of recent trends in philosophy, involves the acquisition of both a new social identity and fluency in a new conceptual language. To this I add a third suggestion: conversion involves a paradigm shift.

Conversion as a Paradigm Shift

If we understand a paradigm as the defining set of beliefs embodied in the life of a community, then a paradigm shift involves for the individual an exchange of allegiance from an old community to a new one. On the level of the community, an individuals aligns with the communal web of belief by participating in the form of communal life that contributes to the telling of a story. For example, humility, which in Aristotle's day was considered a vice rather than a virtue, is urged upon us by New Testament writers as normative for intracommunal relationships precisely because it reflects the self-emptying of Christ, who is our paradigmatic exemplar (Phil. 2:5–8). By treating each other with humility, members of the Christian community become a concrete illustration that enables the world to better understand the story, and thus the identity, of Christ.

On the level of the individual, participation in the community's web of belief functions as an experience decoder, helping the individual recognize and name experiences that might other-wise go unnoticed. Some time ago a psychiatrist friend of mine asked me to meet with one of his patients who showed an inter-est in spiritual things. Frank and I began meeting for coffee and to discuss important writings about spirituality such as Augus-tine's *Confessions* and Kierkegaard's *Purity of Heart*. At one point I asked Frank to read Luke's Gospel. When on the following week I asked him to describe Jesus, he replied that he saw Jesus as a Machiavellian prince, a strong, charismatic individual who built his political movement by preying on the poor, dispossessed, and socially marginalized. I was astonished by Frank's reading because I assumed that of all the Gospels, Luke's portrays Jesus most clearly as the liberator. When I questioned Frank more closely, I learned that his reading was colored by his military upbringing. Son of an army sergeant, Frank equated significance with the sort of machismo that attains power by dominating others. It was only natural for Frank to read Jesus in this light; it was perhaps the only reading Frank could initially give to Luke's Gospel.

Through our conversation, Frank realized that this lens of his military childhood was not bringing the text into proper focus. It dawned on him that a better stance might be to read as if he were one of the poor and dispossessed. Because he suffered from post-traumatic stress disorder, Frank thought that maybe he shared the most in common with the "demonized" persons Jesus had healed and that, therefore, he might fruitfully read *Luke* from that standpoint.

Frank made progress in reading the text rightly by changing the lens through which he read. And a couple of weeks later he changed lenses once again. Ultimately, however, one cannot properly read the Bible until the biblical text ceases to become the object that one views and becomes, instead, the lens itself through which one sees. If this suggestion sounds foreign, it may be because we moderns have fallen out of touch with the pre-dominant reading strategy of the church fathers. This "precrit-ical" reading strategy, in Hans Frei's words, takes Scripture as "Realistic Narrative." This phrase does not mean that we read the Scriptures with a wishful abeyance of sound judgment; sort of a childish "it could happen . . ." mentality. Rather, Frei means that precritical readers took the Scriptures as a narrative that encompassed all reality.[20] According to Frei there are four aspects to this reading.

First, precritical readers took biblical stories as descriptions of actual events. The literal meaning of the story was not simply one piece of evidence for events whose actuality was determined by adding up many strands of evidence. The literal meaning of the text was descriptive of that which could not be described in any other words.

Some time ago I spoke on the phone with a pastor friend who offered the following dichotomy: either the gospel stories are mythical (i.e., fictitious) and have the power to change us only if we act as if they are true, or the gospel stories are historically true. His account is problematic because he fails to see the way treating something as "historically true" treats the gospel accounts as of lesser weight than the nonbiblical evidence upon which the veracity of the gospel "events" supposedly rests. This is a false dichotomy because there is an alternative reading that gives the gospel account the weight appropriately commensurate with its standing as Scripture. Frei suggests that the gospel stories are realistic narratives. Did Jesus walk on water? We can never know if by "know" we mean to have conclusive text-independent evidence. Our only reliable access to this event is through the lens of biblical story. Of course Jesus walked on water. We can vouch for this story precisely because walking on water is just the sort of thing Jesus would do, given the fact that Jesus is the sort of person we understand him to be. What sort of person? The sort of person disclosed by the whole pattern of New Testament stories. Granted, certain stories in the mix may be more difficult than other stories for some to swallow. But a precritical reader was not burdened with straining out the incredible from the credible. Rather, the precritical reader could swallow the less credible story on the basis of its fit with the whole by virtue of the particular stance the reader adopted toward the text as Scripture. As Augustine wrote to Jerome (d. 420 A.D.),

> It is from those books alone of the Scriptures, which are now called canonical, that I have learned to pay them such honor and respect as to believe most firmly that not one of their authors has erred in writing anything at all. If I do find anything in those

books which seems contrary to the truth, I decide that either the text is corrupt, or the translator did not follow what was really said, or that I failed to understand it.[21]

For nonbelievers the biblical text may have simply been a text, but for Augustine the canonical text was Scripture.[22]

Second, it was assumed by precritical readers that the New Testament world was continuous with the world of the Old Testament. That being the case, it is possible to tell the story of the whole of history in a unified and cumulative way. The assumption that there was a narrative unity that tied together all the Old Testament and New Testament episodes gave legitimacy to the use of figural typology for seeing how some parts fit. For example, Augustine says that he was able to embrace Christianity because of the allegorical method used by Ambrose, a method that knit all the disparate parts of Scripture together into a whole.[23] This shows that for the precritical reader, what was really important was the ability of the Scriptures to narrate all reality in a unified way. Their willingness to allegorize some parts of the text does not show disdain for the authority of the text, but a prior and resolute commitment to take the unity of the text literally.

Third, the acknowledgment of continuity between Old Testament and New Testament implied the continuity of the biblical world with the readers' own world: the same world, the same timeline, the same story. Consequently, precritical readers had the tacit responsibility to see themselves in this story: the world of the biblical text is my world, and therefore I must understand and evaluate my life, my ecosystem, my community, and so on, in terms of fit or lack of fit with the biblical story.

Fourth, the meaning of a story cannot be separated from the story itself because there is no non-narrated place to stand to judge the correspondence between the story and its meaning. That is not to say that stories are meaningless or that they are necessarily fanciful. It is just to say that when it comes to stories, we can only get the point of the story by attending to the story. The characters, the plot, and the setting are not ornamental to some deeper point; rather, the point can only be embodied in these concrete particulars. It has been the presumption of modern philosophy that historical records look back upon events and that the critical thinker is burdened with the task of establishing the plausibility of the event by weighing the evidence for and against it. But precritical readers from Ignatius (d. 107) to Calvin (d. 1564) looked *through* the narrative record to view the event. There simply was no other access to the event than the narrative. We can hear this precritical reading strategy echoed in Calvin's words: "For just as the eyes, when dimmed with age or weakness or by some other defect, unless aided by spectacles, discern nothing distinctly; so such is our feebleness, unless Scripture guides us in seeing God, we are immediately confused."[24] It was Calvin's understanding that our eyesight was so poor that the Scriptures could never be considered the sort of glasses that one could see well enough without in order to take off and clean them. Rather, the Scripture is our corrective lens by which everything else is brought into focus.

The upshot of these reading strategies is this: while modern thinkers interrogate the text by subjecting it to historical-critical scrutiny, precritical and postcritical thinkers submit themselves to the text as Scripture in a way that allows the text to interrogate them.

Allow me to summarize the lessons that postcritical philosophy would have us apply to the notion of religious conversion. First, conversion involves a change in social identity. Second, in large measure, this new social identity is accomplished by the acquisition of new language skills. Finally, conversion is constituted by a paradigm shift that results in bringing the world into focus in a whole new way. Notice that in all three cases, conversion involves enculturation into community and into a community of a particular sort. The tracks for being a Christ-follower have already been laid by those who faithfully followed him before us. The conceptual language that the new believer learns to speak has been in circulation for two millennia. Moreover, to say that I have shifted paradigms is but an imprecise way of saying that I have changed allegiance from one community to another. In this light, the gospel is, as it always has been, a radical social challenge to the status quo of individualism.

It does not take much moxie to realize these insights have great significance for the historical practice of evangelism. To this topic we now turn.

3

Evangelism as a Communal Practice

I have outlined three ways in which recent thinking is moving out of the ruts left by three centuries of modern philosophy. In the last chapter I explained that these postmodern, or postcritical, views shed light on the way we understand, from the human side, what happens in religious conversion. In this chapter I suggest that we retool our evangelism according to these insights. This is not intended as a rebuff against those who do evangelism in ways other than those I suggest. On the contrary, the contemporary scene is a mixed bag, and keeping in step with God's Spirit (Gal. 5:25) yields a variety of modes for fitting the gospel to a given context. However, I am concerned that we not overlook the need to contextualize the practice of evangelism for an increasingly postmodern world.

If we take seriously the resources of contemporary philosophy, the practice of evangelism can be enriched in at least three ways. First, our notion of evangelism must be broadened so that we insist on embodying the story in the web of relationships that constitutes our identity. Second, evangelism must engage others in conversations spoken in our conceptual language. And, third, evangelism must enlist the outsider in the telling of the gospel story. Let me unpack these in order.

Embodying the Story

If conversion can be thought of as involving a change in identity, then evangelism must be done in a manner commensurate with our new social identity. We instinctively recognize that the manner in which a message is conveyed must be in harmony with the content of that message. It is easier to get a handle on what this harmony amounts to by considering a negative illustration.

Recently well-intentioned biblical creationists upgraded their arsenal in the bumper-sticker wars with evolutionists. For a time the prominence of the "Jesus fish" was offset by that of bumper stickers championing the very clever "Darwin fish."

Now however, biblical creationists claim to have gotten the upper hand by the introduction of the new and improved Jesus bumper sticker:

"Survival of the Fittest!"

But notice what has happened. The creationists, for good or ill, have given the game away. In their urgency to win the argument, they have legitimized the very subtext that they wish to dispute, for they have made Jesus the biggest fish in evolution's game of one-upmanship.

This illustration shows that style must fit message if a message is not to be self-defeating.[1] The style in which our message is delivered must also be commensurate with the gospel. There are two aspects to the style of evangelism. First, the lone evangelist, who may feel psychologically outnumbered or outgunned, hankers after a method that is irresistible; we want others to be compelled to believe, that they *must* believe the message. But as John Howard Yoder has noted, the *rejectability* of the gospel is ironically what prevents it from becoming mere propaganda.[2] Consequently, the Good News cannot be fully understood as good *news* unless the gospel is offered in noncoercive ways. Stephen's sermon is an example of style-message fit. Whatever you conclude about the rhetoric of his sermon in Acts 7, the authentication of his message came from the manner in which it was delivered. While Stephen's energetic, in-your-face tenor clearly placed him in the line of Old Testament prophets, he stopped short of coercive tactics for persuading his audience. Unexpectedly, he offered his fervent message as a gift and refused to defend himself when the physical attacks came. He neither retaliated against nor imprecated his persecutors. In contrast, he blessed those who cursed him, exemplifying the peculiar manner of the Lord Jesus' response: "Do not hold this sin against them." We see then, that the style of the lone evangelist must match the noncoercive tenor of the Good News.

Second, this principle also holds when the gospel is sung not as a solo but as a choral piece. The characteristic pattern of life of the entire believing community is to its speech what style is to a message. Just as the similarity of Stephen's life to that of Jesus underscored the message he was communicating, so too the way Christians live with each other can powerfully illuminate the Good News. In Paul's first letter to Timothy, he urges him to do the work of an evangelist. Significantly, one way Timothy is to discharge this responsibility is by caring for the quality of life within the local body—because the fit between church's corporate life and its message is crucial to getting the message through. Paul writes, "I am writing you these instructions . . . so that you may know how people ought to conduct themselves in God's household, which is the church of the living God, the pillar and foundation of the truth" (1 Tim. 3:14–15 NIV). Surprisingly, the phrase "pillar and foundation of the truth" modifies "church" rather than "God." In other words, the *church* is the foundation of the truth rather than the other way around. How can this be?

In the main, no sentence can be evaluated as true or false apart from the context that gives the passage its sense. It matters whether it was Billy Graham or Gloria Steinham who said "All men are evil beasts!" By the same token, the world will not be able to evaluate the claims of the gospel unless they understand clearly what is the nature of the community that speaks these claims. The gospel may remain a mystery to the surrounding culture unless the church lives out the gospel in the form of its life together. It is the pattern of the believing community's relationships that embodies the story of Jesus in concrete terms that outsiders can comprehend. Only when the gospel is linked to such concrete illustrations can outsiders say, "I see what you mean." Does a lonely trucker still find Jesus by reading a Gideon Bible in a remote motel room? Of course. I'm not suggesting that the gospel can only be preached by a community. I am saying, rather, that one of the means of God's grace is the body of Christ. Somewhere along the way, the trucker will have met or read about real-McCoy Christians, and that encounter is precisely what gives the gospel enough of a face to be a live option.

My suggestion that the intelligibility of the gospel depends strongly upon the character of the believing community may be disconcerting to Christians who, perhaps because they are steeped in individualism, cannot help but construe evangelism as a matter of one-on-one conversations. I am not advocating that we cease to have face-to-face conversations with individuals about the claim Jesus makes on our lives. Rather, I am suggesting that such conversations will not make complete sense to unbelievers who don't have a clue what difference Jesus makes for the way Christians live with one another. It is praiseworthy that many have labored tirelessly to get the message out despite there appearing to be very little qualitative difference today

between the Christian community and communities of nonbelievers. These laborers hope, of course, that the gospel will be
believed on its own terms, regardless of the mixed messages that
we Christians send by our corporate lives. And we are partly
right to hope for this; hypocrisy among cancer researchers
doesn't invalidate research findings. But sometimes we are
overly optimistic about the punch the gospel packs on its own.
Certain terms of the biblical message are confusing to the nonbeliever, and rather than showing what terms such as *sin,
redemption*, and *resurrection* amount to in the concrete community life, we mistakenly assume that it is the evangelist's job
to *translate* confusing concepts into the language of the unbe-
liever. This strategy is deeply flawed.

In *Two Hundred Years of Theology*, Hendrikus Berkhof chronicles the church's attempt to translate the gospel into terms that
the modern mind can easily grasp. He explains that in 1799
Friedrich Schleiermacher, who has since been dubbed the father
of modern Protestant theology, defended Christianity to a group
of his friends known as the Romantic Circle. In this book, called
On Religion: Speeches to Its Cultured Despisers, Schleiermacher
adopted the strategy of translating the gospel into the vocabulary of romantic philosophy. He saw a common ground between
the romantics' sense of wonder at the power of nature and the
Christian sense of awe-filled dependence on God. Schleiermacher made this notion of "absolute dependence" (*Gefühl*) the
heart and soul of the gospel: what Christians call sin is nothing
but the loss of one's sense of absolute dependence, what makes
Jesus divine is the perfection of his sense of absolute dependence on God, and so on. While we may chastise Schleiermacher
for downplaying, even distorting, what we consider central
tenets of the faith, I want to draw attention to the strategy of his
evangelism. Berkhof asserts that in liberal Protestantism's project of reaching the secular world by expressing the gospel in
terms understandable to the modern mind, the church may be
likened to a boat sailing down the river of time. When the boat
comes upon the shoals of modernity, it must lighten its load to
clear the sandbar. Unfortunately, as the culture becomes increasingly secular, the river becomes ever more shallow, and eventually the church feels forced to unload all its cargo in order to
stay afloat in a secular age! In the words of Alasdair MacIntyre,

"any presentation of theism which is able to secure a hearing from a secular audience has undergone a transformation that has evacuated it entirely of its theistic content."[3] Thus, the most liberal of churches appear able to maintain the best of relations with secular culture, but no longer have anything distinctive to say to it! Righteousness has been reduced to equality, agape has paled to fraternity, sin has been replaced with maladjustment, and salvation has become mere civility.

The failure of liberalism, then, is not one of *intent*—Schleiermacher sincerely wished his friends to embrace Christianity—but one of *strategy*: by attempting to translate the gospel into terms understandable to the modern mind, the liberal wing of the church lost the farm. My fear is that the conservative wing of the church, for all its emphasis on missions, evangelism, and church growth, is simply reproducing an already deeply flawed strategy.

Translation is not the only strategy for communicating the gospel. Sometimes what cannot be plainly spoken may nevertheless be shown. For example, we claim that grace is the very heart of the gospel. Yet the secular mind cannot understand this concept without concrete illustration. You'll remember that I wrote in the last chapter of Frank, whose initial reading misconceived Jesus as a Machiavellian figure who manipulated the poor and dispossessed in order to build his power base. To say the least, Frank was not in a position to understand the term *grace*. But how might the message get through? Surely I could not translate *grace* into terms with which he was already familiar, for grace is unlike anything Frank had ever encountered. What I hoped might work—and I must be honest, to this day Frank still describes himself as distant from Jesus—was the showing of the gospel in the life of our church. I brought Frank to church. He attended a Good Friday service, a men's breakfast, and a baptism celebration. After one of these, he commented on the remarkable spirit of the group, but I sensed that he had a long way to go. Rather than trying to explain grace to him, I told him a story about one of our church's small groups.

Three years ago I had the ultimate "one of those days." We were supposed to spend a family day at the beach, but that morning we received a phone call saying that Jeanne's dad was in the hospital for some testing regarding chest pains. Since nothing more would be known until the test results came back the following morning, we headed for the beach. The rip tide was surprisingly strong, and while swimming with the boys I lost track of eight-year-old Stephen for what seemed to be an eternity. It must have been only ten seconds later when I caught sight of him, panic stricken and laden with kelp, struggling to keep his head above water. I exhausted myself getting to him and getting him to shore. When we arrived home later that night I was grateful to have everyone accounted for and safe in bed. The following morning we learned that Jeanne's dad had been scheduled for sextuple-bypass heart surgery. While she scrambled to get packed, I went outside to get the newspaper, only to discover that our minivan had been stolen in the middle of the night! Within a twenty-four-hour period our child had nearly drowned, our minivan had been stolen, and Jeanne's dad was scheduled for open heart surgery. As I prayed during my devotions that morning, I couldn't suppress the image that I was in a state of emotional free fall. Just as quickly, another image flashed through my mind: that of a safety net provided by God himself. That safety net was our Koinonia Group. Rising from prayer, I called George, our leader, and filled him in. Instantly, the group sprang into action: hot meals were organized for the boys and me for the days Jeanne was gone; five hundred dollars were offered to cover the expense of Jeanne's flight to Minneapolis; and a car was loaned to us for the six weeks that our minivan was missing in action.

What surprised me was Frank's response when I told him the story. He said simply: "What was in it for them?" In other words, Frank's secular mind was so far from understanding grace that he was still waiting for the rest of the story. But what I had told him *was* the whole story. Nothing was in it for them. That's what grace looks like in real life. Frank was speechless—not a bad posture to take when beginning to listen to God.

In attempting to show the gospel to nonbelievers by tracing the character of our believing communities, we are adopting a very ancient evangelistic strategy. The robust character of the early church was commonly the bottom line to which second- and third-century apologists appealed. Consider an example excerpted from a second-century apology written by Aristides to Caesar Hadrian,

> But the Christians . . . show kindness to those near them; and whenever they are judges, they judge uprightly. . . . They do good

to their enemies. . . . If one of them have bondsmen and bondswomen or children, through love towards them they persuade them to become Christians, and when they have done so, they call them brethren without distinction. They do not worship strange gods, and they go their way in all modesty and cheerfulness. Falsehood is not found among them; and they love one another. . . . And he, who has, gives to him who has not, without boasting. And when they see a stranger, they take him in to their own homes and rejoice over him as a very brother. . . . And if they hear that one of their number is imprisoned or afflicted on account of the name of their Messiah, all of them anxiously minister to his necessity. . . . And if there is any among them that is poor and needy, and they have no spare food, they fast two or three days in order to supply to the needy their lack of food. . . .

Such, O King . . . is their manner of life. . . . And verily, this is a new people, and there is something divine in the midst of them.[4]

Apparently Aristides felt that he could not speak of the lasting presence of Emmanuel apart from several pages of text describing the manner in which Christians live with each other. And that is precisely my point: only against the backdrop of a concrete community that resembles Christ, albeit imperfectly, can the gospel be heard most clearly.

The first lesson for evangelism to be gleaned from postcritical philosophy, then, is the importance of embodying the story of Jesus in our communal life. Such a community provides the context that demystifies the gospel by making it concrete.

In many ways this lesson collapses the age-old distinction between evangelism and discipleship. No longer can we afford the specialization that makes some of us evangelists and others of us disciple makers. Rather, to assist believers in resembling Christ on the corporate (and on the individual) level is part and parcel of our Great Commission (see Matt. 28:18–20).

Engaging Others in the Conversation Using Our Language

A second lesson we can learn for evangelism stems from the central role language plays in the conversion process. If conversion involves the acquisition of a new conceptual language, then evangelism must be akin to teaching a foreign language to people who do not yet speak it. George Lindbeck has quipped,

> To the degree that religions are like languages and cultures, they can no more be taught by means of translation than can Chinese or French. What is said in one idiom can to some extent be conveyed in a foreign tongue, but no one learns to understand and speak Chinese by simply hearing and reading translations.[5]

If Lindbeck is correct about this, then evangelism may be very similar to teaching English as a second language. Our problem is, of course, that in our eagerness for others to understand us we are too quick to relieve them of the task of learning to communicate in the new tongue; we so relieve them every time we translate first-order Christian speech into something else. A skeptical philosopher friend who was not unfamiliar with Christianity once asked me how, when I pray, I could address God as "ontologically real in the metaphysical sense." I interrupted him with the question, "Why do you think that translating Christian claims into philosophical-ese makes anything plainer? 'Ontologically real?' 'In the metaphysical sense?' These don't make anything clearer. Rather, we say 'God was in Christ reconciling the world to himself.' We must learn to understand this claim on its own terms."

It remains to be seen whether we can reverse the current trend of biblical illiteracy in our culture. But if it is to be done, it must come by engaging the culture in conversation spoken in *our* language. George Lindbeck urges:

> It is questionable that the churches can seize the opportunities that this [postcritical] intellectual shift provides. . . . Biblical literacy, though not sufficient, is indispensable. This literacy does not consist of historical, critical knowledge about the Bible. Nor does it consist of theological accounts, couched in nonbiblical language, of the Bible's teachings and meanings. Rather it is the patterns and details of its sagas and stories, its images and symbols, its syntax and grammar, which need to be internalized if one is to imagine and think scripturally. . . . What is to be promoted are those approaches which increase familiarity with the text. Even profane close readings of the canonical sources, such as are now becoming popular in a few English literature depart-

ments . . . are to be preferred to theology, however liberating, edifying, or orthodox, which turns attention away from scripture.

Relearning the [conceptual] language of scripture is difficult, and at present there are no signs that the church can do it.[6]

Lindbeck's advice is timely. If the object of evangelism is that outsiders become insiders, and if becoming an insider involves learning a new conceptual language, then we must help others learn to speak by attending to our own familiarity with the living grammar of the text and also by correcting them with utmost patience and good humor as they bungle along groping for words or forming unhappy constructions, because bungling is precisely how one learns to become fluent.

We do this quite naturally with our children. When Danny was four he and I had this conversation:

"Superman is a strong guy!"

"Yes he is, but Jesus is stronger."

"Superman is as strong as Jesus!"

"No, Jesus made Superman [kind of]."

"Superman can turn into real."

"No [backpedaling], Superman is pretend. But even if he were real, Jesus is stronger because Jesus would have made him. Jesus made everything."

"So, Jesus is the strongest?"

"Yep."

"And the angels are the strongest? "

"Uh . . . Yes, but Jesus is stronger than the angels because Jesus made them too."

"Can Jesus make himself?"

Although Danny didn't have the language skills to grapple with the nature of divine action (who among us does!), he did have the language skills to properly rank persons in terms of their respective power. In one sense, Danny's theological maturity progressed by means of learning the truthful way to speak of Jesus in superlative terms: Jesus is the strongest!

We are often tempted to think that theological maturity requires us to have a handle on *explanations* of theological truths. Unfortunately, if explanation were the measure of our maturity, how many of us could pass the test? In the fourth century, St. Gregory of Nazianzus gave this answer to an inquirer: "What is the procession of the Holy Spirit? Do thou tell me first what is the Unbegottenness of the Father and I will explain to you the physiology of the generation of the Son, and the procession of the Spirit—and we shall both of us be frenzy-stricken for prying into the mystery of God."[7] In the absence of an ability to articulate such mysteries, theological orthodoxy has historically contented itself with maintaining the *correct ways to say things*. St. Augustine put it this way:

> We believe that the Father, Son, and Holy Spirit are one God, maker and ruler of every creature, and that the "Father" is not the "Son," nor "Holy Spirit" "Father" or "Son," but a Trinity of mutually related persons, and a unity of equal essence. So let us attempt to understand this truth, praying that he who we wish to understand would help us in doing so, so that we can set out whatever we thus understand with such careful reverence that nothing unworthy is said (even if we sometimes say one thing instead of another). . . . But we must never allow any error to lead us astray in such a way that we *say* something about the Trinity which relates to the creature rather than the Creator, or results from wild speculation.[8]

Augustine doesn't explain the Trinity; he simply urges that we not speak confusedly: on the one hand we rightly say "God is one" and yet we also rightly say "The Father is not the Son (nor the Holy Spirit)." A close study of the church's universal creeds shows them to be grammar lessons, or rules for proper ways of speaking.

Of course, orthodoxy is more than mere words. As postmodern philosophy of language teaches us, becoming fluent in a language involves participation in the grammar of the language, that is, participation in the form of life of the language's speakers. (Part of what *chair* means is sitting in one.) Thus, to become fluent in the conceptual language that Christians speak is to participate in activities such as forgiving one's neighbor, giving thanks to God, and worshiping with other believers.

On the other hand, orthodoxy is never less than words. Words have never been accidental to Christian theology. Wittgenstein may have emphasized the givenness of shared human activity for the learning of language when he quoted Goethe: "In the beginning was the act." But Christians could never put it that way. We see the linguistic character of all created reality as something God-endowed, for we confess with the apostle, "In the beginning was the Word."

So then, I am not saying that nonbelievers are turned into believers by our simply teaching them the right things to say. That's ridiculous; a scholar's parrot may talk Greek. Rather, I am saying that conversion is incomplete apart from learning the conceptual language of Christianity. We serve others most lovingly by engaging them in conversations spoken in our tongue because, as any language instructor will tell you, languages are most completely internalized when the new speaker learns the language by immersion. When I taught in Russia, I was terrified of the prospect of a six-hour layover in Frankfurt, Germany. In Russia I would always have a translator by my side, but what was I going to do on my own in Germany? My fear was unfounded, for whether they liked to or not, everyone in Frankfurt accommodated me by speaking to me—the dumb foreigner—in English. Of course, that didn't help me improve my German. Only if I had had no recourse to speaking English and had been entirely surrounded by native speakers would I have been able to pick up some of their language. I would have had two weeks to figure out names of basic foodstuffs before I starved; less than three days to learn "water"; and only minutes to learn how to say "bathroom"!

We Christians, then, must become the linguistic culture into which nonbelievers become immersed—perhaps not of their own willing, but of ours—by our engaging them in conversations using our native language.

Enlisting Potential Converts in the Telling of the Story

A third implication for evangelism follows directly from the notion that conversion involves a paradigm shift. But in order to get there, I must say a bit more about paradigms.

Because paradigms are corporate property, to participate in a paradigm shift involves transferring one's allegiance from one community to another. Unfortunately, a culture's default paradigm, what we might call the regnant paradigm, is typically so pervasive, and the community that holds it is so broad, that the paradigm is virtually invisible—even to its own members. One typical objection to the work of proponents of paradigm theory (such as Thomas Kuhn and Alasdair MacIntyre) is that we all obviously inhabit a variety of communities rather than a single community. According to paradigm theory, must we not therefore share in a variety of paradigms rather than a single homogenous, monolithic paradigm? And if that is the case, then can it still be said that paradigms shift in revolutionary ways?

This objection may imagine paradigms in ways smaller than envisioned by Kuhn or MacIntyre. We can dissolve this challenge by observing the nature of verbal paradigms. When we conjugate regular verbs, the paradigm names the rules according to which the verb forms change. For example, the similarity is unmistakable between the present tense forms of the Latin verbs "to praise"(laudo, laudas, laudat, laudamus, laudatis, laudant—I praise, you praise, he-she-it praises, we praise, you [plural] praise, they praise) and "to arouse" (incito, incitas, incitat, incitamus, incitatis, incitant). Are these the same words? Of course not. And yet they are similar. We might say that these two verbs are conjugated by the same rule-governed procedure. Or we might say that there is a family resemblance between these regular verbs. This similarity is called "the verbal paradigm." It is true that we all simultaneously inhabit a number of communities. However, it is questionable whether each identifiable community is the sole possessor of a unique paradigm. In a way analogous to verbal paradigms, there may be a resemblance that unites all the disparate local communities of which one is a part by providing the rules by which the game called community life is played. If so, then these rules define the paradigm lurking just below the surface.

Growing up in Minnesota, my wife and I were simultaneously members of several communities: a neighborhood with a particular ethnic and religious demography; an extended family with aunts and uncles; the township of Richfield, which boasted of great drinking water and a champion high school soccer team; the state of Minnesota, which was politically to the left of my extended family; and so on. Yet these disparate communities shared an ethos that might be called consumerism.[9] Members of all groups of which we were members prized education for its ability to help one "get ahead." Strictly speaking, getting ahead was not simply a matter of financial ease; affluence was always the by-product of a greater good: an increased power to choose. The goal wasn't having money but having the *option* to accumulate money, or to move across town, or to start an new business, or to become a missionary if one so chose. I imagine that my fundamentalist relatives would not automatically label themselves as "consumers"; nor would the people of the township of Richfield feel comfortable being lumped together in the same category as my relatives! And yet it was consumerism— the drive to expand personal options—that described the underlying regularity of the life that was played out within and between these diverse groups.

In large measure, the family resemblance that defines community life in this broader sense goes unnoticed. In Copernicus's day there were undoubtedly merchants and serfs and aristocrats who would have nothing to do with each other. But they were all Ptolemaists. Not that those who first heard Copernicus's theory were likely to have identified themselves as Ptolemaists. (Surely some of them could not have even spelled *Ptolemaist*!) Rather, they would have simply taken for granted that the earth was at the center of the universe and that Copernicus was just plain nuts. However, what is shared among Ptolemaists, or what is shared among consumers, is a way of viewing the world, a paradigm that is so pervasive and deeply embedded that it is simply taken for granted.

More important for my purpose is the difference between being a Ptolemaist and being a consumer. Being a Ptolemaist had little to do with how one treated one's neighbor, but being a consumer has everything to do with the way we live with one another. Christianity offers a rival paradigm in this second sense. But I am getting ahead of myself.

So the criteria for evaluating a conceptual paradigm are internal to, and thus supportive of, the nearly invisible regnant paradigm itself. This poses a problem for our task of persuading others. How can persuasion be accomplished? What might drive someone into close enough proximity with a patently nutty community in order that the rationality of that community might rub off? There are several possibilities.

First, desperation drives some to shop around. Sometimes people get a hunch that their community's way of living and thinking has or will soon hit a dead end. For example, Newtonian physics simply could not explain why high-speed particles behave as they do. The Newtonian paradigm's only chance of remaining viable was if it faced and overcame the epistemological crisis presented by this problem. Had Newton's guild possessed the resources for overcoming the crisis, the Newtonian paradigm would have been strengthened, and so too the community's commitment to it. But precisely because such resources were lacking, a new paradigm—in this case quantum physics—emerged as the winner.[10]

A second factor can motivate outsiders to investigate a community that is constituted by an alternative paradigm: curiosity. While the paradigm of the status quo may be invisible because it is embodied at every level of social life, the alien community is identifiable precisely because of its stark contrast with the status quo. In Aristides' apology cited above, it is clear that something divine was recognizable in the unearthly way Christians treated each other. Why, St. Clement of Rome wrote about Christians who sold themselves into slavery in order to ransom others or to feed the poor![11] How curious!

Third, a friendship formed with an insider of a rival community may be the handrail that assists one's ascent into the new community. Friendship can be thought of as the embodiment of conversation: the character and durability of a conversation *is* the character and durability of the friendship. So the question becomes: am I, as the evangelist, able to sustain dialogue with my nonbelieving friend long enough?

An affirmative answer to this question requires what Nietzsche (in a vastly different context) called "long obedience in the same direction." For to acknowledge that conversion involves the shifting of a paradigm is to also acknowledge that the persuasion of my friend will happen not incrementally, but all at once. In other words, because beliefs come in interlocking sets, I cannot expect my friend to surrender beliefs one at a time until conversion is complete. Rather, it is likely that I will see virtually no progress in the conversation apart from a growing tension—even irritability—on the part of my friend whose paradigm has been set in dissonance by the rival story of Jesus. Now the question is whether I am willing to endure, even augment, this tension until the Gestalt switch of conversion occurs. Typically, I become discouraged by the mounting tension and foolishly move on to "riper fruit" at just about the time "the light dawns over the whole."[12]

So how do we keep the conversation going? Recall that the use of language as postcritical thinkers have explained it has wide practical ramifications. Our use of language—our conversation—is not simply a matter of the words we bandy about over cups of coffee. Rather, fluent use of a conceptual language involves participation in a community's defining form of life. Thus to speak about God intelligibly requires participation in such activities as confession, worship, and thanksgiving. It follows that a rich conversation with a friend necessarily involves the friend's participation with us in these activities. Then our conversation will be carried on at more than one level and from more than one stance. On a cursory level, words are being exchanged. But there is also a tacit conversation that is carried on at a more profound level of activity. For example, I might have a commitment to serve at a shelter for homeless people in my area. In doing so, I am contributing to the telling of the story of Jesus; this might even be called incarnational evangelism since the gospel message is as loudly spoken in these actions as it might be spoken in words. Now if I bring my friend, who serves alongside of me, my friend is, according to Matthew 25, also speaking for Jesus and to Jesus in these same concrete acts of kindness. It is easy to imagine that repeated trips to a soup kitchen might cure money grubbers of their materialism and implant compassion in the hardest of hearts. So too, participation in Jesus-like social action is persuasive at a very deep level for participants of all shades of prior commitment.

Additionally the *stance* my friend takes in serving homeless persons is itself more akin to that taken by Jesus than that taken by a nonbeliever. In other words, for that hour in the soup kitchen my friend "speaks" as if an insider. Not only are the friend's actions amenable to the gospel message, my friend is actually acting as an advocate for the gospel—even while simply scooping potatoes. The increased persuasive power of the gospel upon the not-yet-believing friend is the result both of carrying on the conversation at a tacit level (i.e., embodying Christlike action) and the switching, temporarily at least, of his or her stance in the conversation (i.e., as an advocate rather than a seeker). The real test will be the development of the friend's own description of what they are doing when they scoop potatoes. "Helping out at the homeless shelter" is a promising beginning, "Trying to impress an attractive co-worker" is not.

My neighbor across the street—let's call him Bill—has been converting to Christianity for the past three years. I met the "new and improved" Bill at the end of period of great turmoil in his life. He and his common-law wife had been drug addicts. He had left his mate and gained custody of their son. He had landed a job, but the physical demands of kicking amphetamines required him to sleep during most of his off hours for the first few months. The days crept by. When I met Bill, he was sleeping better and had just decided to quit smoking and begin exercising. I figured "getting religion" would be the logical next step in Bill's self-help program. So I invited Bill to come to church. First he attended a children's musical (our kids play together). Then he began attending worship. Somewhere along the line I gave him a Bible, which he undertook to read cover to cover. On Sundays I watched in amazement as he learned to sing songs of worship. Now, it has been said that more lies are spoken over the cover of a hymnal than anywhere else on the planet. But Bill's tuneful worship was not self-deceiving; rather, it was a training to see life under the aspect of the gospel, a learning to see things as they really are. In time, Bill was baptized and publicly gave as clear a presentation of his journey to Christ as he was able to muster at his level of understanding. He also began meeting with a small group in our church. Somewhere in this process of conversion, Bill was no longer self-helping himself into religion. Instead, he had learned to correctly see himself as the recipient of an undeserved and saving grace.

Bill's process of conversion cannot be distilled into a linear cause-and-effect chain that could be programmed for just about anyone. What took place in Bill's life was involvement in a conversation. Initially, Bill participated as a recipient: he heard the gospel embodied in the kids' musical, in the preaching of sermons, in the prayers of others; he read the text as a recipient of a notable message. He also shifted his stance to participate in the conversation as an advocate: he sang songs as unto God; he gave a personal testimony before his baptism; he incarnated the gospel in miniature in the enactment of his baptism; he participated with the rest of the body of Christ in incarnating the story of remembrance we call Eucharist; he participated in acts of charity and care for his fellow believers through the ministry of our small group.

My point is not to create a new formula for doing evangelism, but to help you, my reader, see evangelism in a different way. I am suggesting that recent trends in philosophy may give us the resources to do ministry in general, and evangelism in particular, in ways that better fit our postmodern world. Because conversion involves a change in social identity, evangelism must be a corporate practice, executed by the community that is the source of the believer's new identity. Second, because conversion involves the acquisition of a new conceptual language, evangelism must engage outsiders in conversations spoken in that language. Third, because conversion involves a paradigm shift, evangelism must seek to assist that shift by being dialogical in style and by, wherever possible, enlisting potential converts in the telling of the story.

These recent trends also give us resources for detecting the Spirit's work among and through Christ's people. In the next two chapters we will examine five stories about evangelism, conversion, and discipleship in order to clothe the philosophical concepts in more tangible arguments.

4

Taking Time
for Fluency

The average tenure of a youth pastor is shockingly short. The last figure I read placed it at less than three years. Granted, there are many factors that contribute to this instability. Some find youth ministry an impossible tightrope; they are expected to live in a manner that reassures the senior pastor and the parents (whose children they are supposed to salvage from the clutches of rebelliousness) and yet live in a way that is sufficiently anti-establishment to win the trust and admiration of the younger generation. Others become weary of the pace of youth ministry: an evening outreach that begins with an exhausting game of capture the flag or a deafening concert by a Christian rock band may end up—if all goes well!—with an intense evangelistic discussion over a midnight pizza facilitated by the very person who is required to attend the predawn prayer meeting with the rest of the church staff. And of course the vitality that comes from being twenty-something has its own peculiar downside: the vast majority of youth ministers are poised on the brink of major life changes—seminary, marriage, children—which may dilute their accessibility by teens, thus their relevance, thus their effectiveness, and thus their longevity. And one problem remains particularly daunting for even the most stout-hearted and relationally savvy: How is a youth pastor to reach a *postmodern* generation, a generation the likes of which has never been seen before?

This question lends irony to my experience at a recent youth ministry conference. Over meals I heard many astonishing stories of how young people were coming to faith in highly unconventional ways. Knowing that contemporary youth ministry is a different animal than the horse that went by the same name twenty years ago, the conference organizers, themselves forty-something, wisely avoided bringing in as plenary speakers typical church-growth cheerleaders and opted instead to bring in professional Christian philosophers to help unknot the tangle of questions embedded in the minds of those who sought to reach the contemporary world. Here lies the irony: by their own admission, these philosophers, each at midlife or beyond, had virtually no direct experience in ministering to the culture in question, while the audience was packed with those who had just such experience. The philosophers' own postmodern views were attained after careful and painful surrender of their modern schooling, while those in the audience had absolutely no qualms about trading Descartes for Wittgenstein, having never heard of either, and spoke postmodernese with great fluency. So the sessions progressed something like this: the philosophers speculated aloud as to how ministry ought to work given what they understood of postmodernity, while the conferees were left to pick and choose haphazardly what bits and pieces struck them as most promising for their future ministry.

I wondered if things shouldn't have been reversed. It seems to me that the conferees ought to have been the main speakers. The stories that emerged around shared meals would have provided wonderful clues to the way God's Spirit is at work in this new generation. If philosophers had a role to play at all it should have been to help trace the grammar of these experiences, pointing out which aspects were genuinely postmodern and at the same time authentically Christian. In what follows, I attempt just such a reversed procedure. I do not pretend that the five stories I will recount will be in any way normative or paradigmatic for the mode of postmodern ministry.[1] But I want to use these stories as the data for which the postmodern categories discussed in the last three chapters make sense. Perhaps we'll even discover that this new conceptual language changes our expectations of what counts as ministry excellence and shows us the way forward. While postmodern self-descriptions come most naturally to those under 25, the evidence that we may be entering a new age is shown by the increasing ease with which postmodern descriptions fit the experience of those older than 25. In the present chapter we will trace the faith journeys of Doreen (a tenured professor of English), Larry (a retired man dying of cancer), and Heidi (a high school student). Doreen's story will remind us that conversion is a timeful process. Larry's story underscores the need to learn Christianity as one would learn a language by immersion. And Heidi's story shows the role that catechesis may play in the conversion process.

Taking Time: Doreen

Doreen[2] first began attending Cedar Ridge Community Church outside Baltimore two years ago when she decided to tag along with her neighbors. They were such genuinely good people that after watching them for a year, Doreen decided that she wanted to go to whatever church they went to.

After hearing her first sermon at CCRC, she confronted the pastor: "This was my first Sunday here. I really disagreed with a couple things you said." After complaining for a minute and finding the pastor, Brian McLaren, surprisingly nondefensive, Doreen quickly backpedaled, "On the whole I really liked it. I could imagine getting involved here. Not just coming, but really getting involved. But you know, I'm a Buddhist. I'm not a Christian. Can't stand 'born-agains,' but is that okay? Can I really get involved here?"

McLaren responded, "Sure. I'd love to have you get involved, unless of course you want to come here and convert people to Buddhism. You wouldn't want me to go to a Buddhist meeting and try to convert people.

But if you're saying that you simply want to be part of the community, then that's great. By the way, I'm really interested in your Buddhist commitment. I'd love to hear about that some time. Why don't we get lunch sometime?"

Doreen was surprised when McLaren called a few days later to pursue their conversation. She later told McLaren over the phone, "I was shocked! I was almost certain that you were just being polite when you said you wanted to hear about my background." It was five weeks later when the two were able finally to schedule a meeting. But during the intervening weeks she was at CCRC on four out of the five Sundays. (The one Sunday she wasn't there she had called the church office leaving a message apologizing for her absence!) When they met in person, Doreen began by apologizing for the tone she had taken towards his sermon in their initial conversation. Sheepishly she admitted, "Look, I told you I'm a Buddhist. But my Buddhism is really shallow. It was just my excuse. I've been coming to church for these last few weeks, and all I want to do is know God. I started praying. Buddhists aren't supposed to pray! But I started praying. The tree in my front yard is dying. I felt so sorry for it. I've been praying for the tree. Is that okay?"

Doreen kept coming. And she started to get involved, though she half-expected at any moment to be cornered by some fanatic intent on clobbering her with wild-eyed speculations about the inner workings of the Trinity or worse. But her quest to become a follower of Jesus steadily progressed. Four months after her initial visit, the associate pastor, Robert, preached a sermon that arrested her attention. She raced over to McLaren at the end of the service: "Wasn't that fantastic? That was just great!" McLaren agreed that Robert had done a good job. "No, no, no. Not that. That thing he read from St. John." McLaren remembered that Robert had quoted in passing a verse from John 17. Doreen explained: "Remember that thing Jesus said, that he was in God and God was in Jesus? That's been my problem; I couldn't believe in Jesus. But when I heard him read that, I thought 'I can believe that!'"

Six or eight months later, McLaren preached a sermon and somewhere in the sermon talked about the fatherhood of God. After the service Doreen confided to him, "I wept during your message. Usually when I hear anyone talk about the subject of God as father I think of all the evils of patriarchalism. Today for the first time I got the idea. What a really cool idea it is that God as a father could love me."

While it took Doreen two years to join a small group, and it is not clear whether her doctrinal stance is yet up to evangelical snuff, her newfound faith is leaking into her life in profound ways. As a tenured professor of English literature, Doreen has been thoroughly schooled in literary theories whose aim it is to expose the darker agendas presumed to be lurking behind any religious practice or language. Yet she confessed to McLaren, "This church is really messing me up. I was finished with my next novel. Now, I have to rewrite the whole thing on account of my main character. I thought I had this really well-developed character. But this character has no spirituality. And I'm thinking, 'Why write a book in which there is no spirituality?'!"

What is striking about Doreen's story is the ambiguity that surrounds the "moment" of her conversion. Many people think that there must be an instant in time when Doreen entered the kingdom (What if she had been in a plane crash a moment too soon?), but her pastor is untroubled by the fact that there is no single point of time that Doreen can identify as the moment of her salvation. McLaren explains:

> We don't do "sinner's prayers" at CRCC or make a big deal about "When did you 'get saved?'" The whole language of punctiliar salvation is problematic for ministry in a postmodern context, I think. Instead, we talk about becoming followers of Christ. We're very reticent about using evangelical jargon, not just because we think it's easily misunderstood, but also because we think it is often sub-biblical in its modernism.

McLaren makes a good point. There is a temptation to think of conversion as something that can be explained in a quasi-mechanical way. We look for causes of conversion (e.g., intercession, hearing the Word of God, a divinely appointed crisis), attempt to specify the moment of decision, and then seek to trace the effects of the decision as if the actions are logically distinct and temporally subsequent by-products of the presumably private, interior act of deciding. Some systematic theologians go so far as to spell out the logical progression of salvation.[3] Perhaps those accounts are persuasive in part because we tend to overlook the Hebrew concept of repentance as a turning (*shūv*) in favor of the light-switch metaphor that we commonly associate with the Greek concept of repentance as a change of mind (*metanoia*). While I do not wish to settle which concept of conversion is more apt on lexical grounds, it may be instructive to note that the earliest Christians commonly treated conversion as time intensive. Hints that new believers had a transitional status can be seen in the writings of both John (e.g., the language of children, fathers, young people in 1 John) and Paul (e.g., Paul suspended evangelistic preaching in favor of providing a year and a half of theological education for recent converts in the home of Titus Justus; Acts 18:7–11). Augustine himself converted from Neoplatonic philosophy to Christianity over a period of three years.[4] In the third century, Hippolytus reported that catechesis commonly lasted for an entire year and sometimes up to three years.[5]

Interestingly, non-Western cultures have had an easier time embracing the notion of progressive conversion than Western culture has.[6] This can be seen in a painting by Korean artist Kim Hak Soo, whose depiction of the Sermon on the Mount shows Jesus in a place of prominence, but above and to the left of the painting's center, as if the entire scene is viewed through the eyes of one who has not yet decided where to stand.[7] The rolling hills and the slightly tangential path leading up the hill give the impression that the artist sees the route to Jesus as neither straightforward nor easy. Questions about which persons are in and which are out—terms in which the question of salvation is commonly framed in the West—are almost beside the point. Rather, the artist's uneven path cluttered with groups of people and even whole families suggests different key questions. What group are you with? How close is your group to the center, to Jesus? Is your group moving toward Jesus or will your group bypass him?

Doreen's story epitomizes the way our postmodern era reveals conversion to be a time-consuming—and time-redeeming—process. Recent philosophy has prepared us to understand why conversion might be so. If beliefs come in weblike sets, and if conversion is the wholesale exchange of one belief-set for another of an entirely different order, that is, a paradigm shift, then it is not surprising that an exchange of such magnitude is not likely to be accomplished overnight. Not only is it likely that the evangelistic conversations that lead up to such a shift will be time-consuming for both parties, the abandonment of one set of beliefs and the construction of a new set will certainly be no straightforward task either. As we shall see in our next story, conversion is a process because it involves progress toward fluency in a whole new language.

Why do some find ambiguity about the timetable of conversion troubling, even threatening? McLaren speculates that such fear

> has to do with the way postmodernity has opened us to questions that we couldn't ask back when everything was working so well. Here's the way I put it: The gospel is too often a story about how people can go to heaven rather than hell when they die. But I think we've got to realize that that isn't what the gospel is really about. The gospel isn't about how Jesus saves individual souls from hell. The gospel is about how Jesus saves the world.

There was a time in our recent past when our culture seemed to assist the conversion of would-be Christ-followers. In the mid-twentieth century, church attendance was commonplace and biblical literacy was high. For citizens of such an age, who already had more than an inkling of the identity of the Christian God and the role of Jesus in salvation, conversion seemed only to entail the correction of a few key beliefs—perhaps learning that salvation is by grace rather than works. The mid-twentieth century saw an explosion in the number of parachurch organizations designed to enflame churches with evangelistic zeal. The techniques that emerged for spreading the gospel in this context shared two important features. First, evangelism was taken to be a relatively straightforward and simple task: communicate the propositions of the gospel, identify the listener's errant beliefs, and challenge the listener to adopt correct beliefs. Second, association with a church body was encouraged, but only as a step subsequent to the decision for Christ. Of course, in an age when the civility of one's immediate family, workplace, and neighborhood was still a fair approximation of the Golden Rule, the urgency for the convert to exchange communities was not readily felt. The upshot of these two features is that evangelism was plagued by an individualism of the most tenacious sort. Even many church services, precisely because they aim at being seeker-sensitive, reflected and still reflect an individualistic approach to evangelism. McLaren explains:

> We at CRCC also struggle with a lot of song lyrics for "worship songs." So many of them are almost spiritually hedonistic: how good Jesus makes *me* feel, what he does for *me*, blah blah blah. I'm all for spiritual experience, but I think we drift into a kind of spiritual narcissism, which is a turn-off for postmodern people, who seem more attuned to issues of social justice than the average evangelical.

McLaren's observation about the ear that postmoderns have toward issues of social justice is not evidence that postmoderns are more altruistic or noble than former generations. Rather, they no longer see the world from the perspective of the isolated individual. And this affords a great opportunity for Christians to correct the way we present the gospel. Saving the whole world involves the reproduction of a pattern of relationships that requires many more than one person. (One cannot be truly forbearing alone on a desert island!) This pattern of interpersonal relationships has no secular analog. It is as unique as the cross of Christ after which it is modeled. Because of the importance of maintaining the integrity of this weave of relationships, an individual's conversion cannot be considered completed until he or she is seamlessly woven into the fabric of the believing community. This is what makes conversion so time-intensive. Salvation may be more than adoption and socialization into this new family's radical way of life, but it is certainly not less.

Of course, standing in a garage doesn't make one a car. Then doesn't it stand to reason that going to church cannot make one a Christian? Yet this objection obscures the truth in Doreen's case: participation in the life of the church *does* make one a participant in the Life of the church. By "life," I mean more than a set of activities and practices. The life of the church is necessarily the presence of the Holy Spirit in the midst of the day-to-day hurly-burly of the believing community.[8] Such a presence cannot be conceived apart from the manner in which Christians actually treat each other. If a believing community is marked by love, forgiveness, generosity, love for God's Word, and faithfulness, we say that the Spirit is present. When these characteristics are missing, we say that the Spirit is, in some sense at least, absent.

And rightly so. In making such a judgment we show that the living presence of the Spirit in a believing community and the shape of intracommunal relationships are internally related. In other words, neither the Spirit's presence nor the community's form of life can be conceived or spoken of without the other set of concepts close at hand. In order to properly emphasize how radically distinctive Christian social life is meant to be, we assert that it cannot be imitated by secular society because, after all, what makes it distinctive is the living presence of God's Spirit.[9] In order to explain the difference that the Spirit's presence makes, we must resort to describing the very behaviors that typify the authentic Christian living that we were trying to explain in the first place!

Does the inseparable relationship between descriptions of Christian behavior and of the presence of the Spirit leave the meanings of both ambiguous? Maybe. But if so, such ambiguity ought not trouble us, for the New Testament often uses double entendre to express the significance of two interrelated notions. For example, John's Gospel reports:"Jesus said to them, 'I tell you the truth. . . . Whoever eats my flesh and drinks my blood remains in me, and I in him.' . . . On hearing it, many of his disciples said, 'This is a hard teaching. Who can accept it?'" (John 6:53–60 NIV).

There is a close connection between eating Jesus' flesh and blood and remaining in him. We rightly understand that remaining in him is something good, as in staying close to Jesus. But what does it mean to eat his flesh? Of course, it cannot mean eating his literal body—no one can do that anyway, because Jesus is resurrected. Can we say that simply partaking of the Lord's Table, the Eucharist, is sufficient to guarantee vital fellowship with the Savior. That would be mere magic.[10] What then can eating his flesh mean?

Maybe we are looking at the problem the wrong way around. In other words, maybe the problem isn't with the word "eating" but with the word "in." Maybe eating his flesh *is* simply the

Eucharistic meal but simple participation does not result in vital fellowship. Instead, right participation is a *symptom* of remaining in Jesus. Why use the spatial preposition *in* rather than *with*? While we cannot speculate about why Jesus used one word rather than another, we do know that the early church's practice of reading John's Gospel (A.D. 90) was heavily influenced by the Pauline literature that had been circulating for at least twenty years before the fourth Gospel was penned. Surely anyone familiar with the Corinthian correspondence would have understood that being *in* Christ was of a piece with being *in* the body of Christ: "Now you are the body of Christ and individually members of it" (1 Cor. 12:27 NRSV). The body of believers is the physical community, thus the phrase "remains in me" is a description of those who stand in vital fellowship with others in the believing community. In sum, Jesus' words were a solemn reminder that following him meant publicly throwing in one's lot with those who celebrated the Lord's Table knowing that their commemoration of Christ's death might prefigure their own martyrdom. Before Constantine legalized Christianity in A.D. 315, it was inconceivable that one could separate the notion of one's personal relationship with Christ from the notion of one's place in the believing community. People did not trifle with playacting conversion when fraternizing with "people of the Way" might cost one's life.

So then, we must rid our minds of the artificial dilemma posed between individual faith and community involvement. Neither is logically prior to the other, because they are two sides of the same coin. Thus, Doreen's conversion was time-consuming because conversion was nothing less than becoming an integral part of a believing community.

This way of putting things may shed light on very perplexing questions about the salvation of the people with developmental disabilities. These questions arise in part because developmentally disabled folk lie outside the reach of modern methods of evangelism. One of my closest friends and his wife are medical doctors, psychiatrists to be exact. Two of their children are very bright. And then there is Sam. Sam is a highly functional autistic boy. His level of development puts him at the awkward boundary where mainstreaming is hoped for, but always slightly out of reach. Sam has excellent concrete math skills, but his ability to grasp abstract concepts is virtually nil. He is a sweet and loving boy but lacks the ability to read interpersonal cues that for the rest of us trigger empathy, pity, and so on.

Sam's inability to grasp the abstract leads to the obvious question: If an understanding of the propositions of the gospel is necessary for saving faith, on what grounds can Sam be saved?[11] One approach to this question has been to assert that persons with autism and other developmental disabilities, as well as those who are stillborn or aborted or die in infancy, are an exception to the general rule that salvation requires individual assent to the propositions of the gospel.[12]

Another approach challenges the assumption that saving faith is necessarily propositional.[13] If it were, those who could not grasp abstract propositions such as "Jesus died for me" could not be saved because the necessary intellectual component of faith would be defective. But what if the intellectual component of faith (held by many to be necessary to saving faith) was exercised corporately rather than by individuals per se? Long ago a theological distinction was made between personal faith (*fides propria*) and implicit faith (*fides implicita*). Personal faith is the explicit trust that I as an individual agent place in an object, such as God and the promises of his Word. Implicit faith signifies the trust one places in others who have a clearer grasp on the trustworthiness of an object. This distinction may help us understand to what extent Sam's inclusion in the believing community may constitute saving faith for him, despite his inability to conceptualize abstract propositions. If faith is always to some degree implicit, then Sam's faith may differ from ours in degree rather than kind.

I am from Minnesota, and I have no qualms about striding out onto a frozen lake in mid-January. I have direct experience with ice and Minnesota winters, and am reasonably familiar with the reliability of the phase change that H_2O undergoes at subfreezing temperatures. A visitor from the tropics may stride after me boldly under the mistaken impression that we are crossing a snow-covered field, and boldness may turn to panic when we pass a fisherman pulling a fish from a hole in the ice. My friend's comprehension of the situation is badly mistaken, but I am a trustworthy guide, and my friend is safe. A similar argument might be made for those who, like Sam, are unable to think clearly about whom or what they are trusting or even understand that what they are doing is called trusting.

I must be clear. I am not saying that Sam is saved simply by virtue of having needs that he cannot conceptualize, let alone meet. I am saying that his vulnerability and weakness do not lead him to ruin, because Sam is numbered among those saved ones who care for him. Others' care for Sam (that of both his immediate family and the believing congregation as a whole) is an expression of *their* saving faith. This sort of community—a community that cares for poor and marginalized and weak and sick and disabled people—is precisely part of the gift of salvation that God has given to a lost world.[14]

If faith is implicit and salvation is associative for people like Sam, then a surprising mark of their salvation is that they will be unaware of it. In the second way of thinking about faith that I have sketched, salvific power extends from the community that explicitly exercises faith to those who are unable to cognize faith at all and yet are properly understood as insiders of the community of faith. Granted, much more work needs to be done on the concept of insiders. But consider this: the church fathers insisted that outside the church there was no salvation (*ad extra ecclesiam nulla salus*) because participation in the life-giving and salvation-conveying Spirit of God could not be understood apart from direct participation in the life of the believing community. Did they think that participation in the believing community could be passive as well as active? Maybe. In the present case, one of the distinctive marks of the believing community is the sort of activity they undertake in caring for persons like Sam. Without persons like Sam in the mix, relations within the believing community would be no more extraordinary than the garden variety decency one encounters in civil society at its best. But the distinctive identity of Christ-followers comes to light when strangers such as Sam are welcomed as friends. In fact, the corporate persona of the believing community as Christlike *requires* direct contact with needy persons such as Sam. Without the Sams of the world, such a community cannot fully embody the Good News about Emmanuel. And if it does not fully embody the Good News, are its members exempt from the surprise ending of Jesus' parable in Matthew 25:31–46? So the salvation of the community may be as dependent on the inclusion of Sam as Sam's salvation is on their inclusion of him.

Now I must be clear, the Reformers denied that implicit faith could save. So insistent were they that when they talked about implicit faith they sometimes preferred to use the pejorative *fides carbonaria*—"faith in the charcoal burner"—to mock those who seemed to think that high-church ritual was a trustworthy object of faith. And in their medieval context, considering the horrific excesses, such as the sale of indulgences, by which "implicit faith" resulted in personal irresponsibility and *un*faith, their denial is entirely understandable. Nevertheless, one wonders if the Reformers' denial ought to have been so categorical. If conversion is about making insiders out of outsiders, then perhaps we needn't fear on account of Sam's cognitive inability so long as Sam's community keeps the faith toward him by its robust imitation of Christ.[15]

Doreen's story fires our imagination to consider conversion as time-consuming because it is inherently social. Such sociality does not operate in exclusion of personal faith. Rather, personal faith is incomplete without socialization because faith always has an implicit dimension. In the next story, we see that part and parcel of the conversion-as-socialization process is learning to speak a new language.

Fluency by Immersion: Larry

Teresa saw a car for sale outside the neighborhood health food store.[16] The owner was Doug Pagitt, pastor of Solomon's Porch, an unusual church that meets in a second-floor loft in a section of Minneapolis that is undergoing restoration. When Teresa went to Solomon's Porch to pick up the keys, she was astonished by the large room littered with easy chairs and couches that formed a loose circle around what appeared to be an altar. "What is this place?" she asked. When Pagitt explained that it was a church, Teresa replied, "I could go to a church like this!"

Teresa's partner, Larry, was in his early sixties and battling cancer. Part of his therapy—both mental and physical—was regular exercise. Teresa suggested to Larry that he join a group from Solomon's Porch that walks around one of the city's lakes. As they walk, pairs of people typically share prayer requests and pray conversationally for each other.

On his first night Larry was paired with Pagitt. He blurted out, "I got this cancer in my lungs and I want to drive this little f– – –er right out. Excuse me, I don't know how to pray yet."

Pagitt recalls that night as the occasion of Larry's first lesson in Christian prayer:

> I didn't care what words he was using, by them he was trying to engage in spiritual warfare. Prayer is combat. He could understand that, because he had been through radiation and chemotherapy and knew that he was at war. But he was new to prayer, so for his sake I prayed in the simplest terms: "Lord, I pray for Larry, I pray for his cancer." Our prayer together that night was very ordinary, very conversational. Obviously, we were walking, so our eyes weren't shut. But I reached over and squeezed him on his shoulder. My head was bowed slightly, and his was too; he seemed to be deliberately assuming the "posture" of prayer. I don't remember all the words he used, but he spoke simply, albeit awkwardly, as if he were an adolescent talking to an adult. He muddled along, "Help me, and be with Teresa and be with Lilly [his daughter]." Larry came to us as someone steeped in Native American spiritualism. But that night he was working hard to pray in our language, perhaps in part to make me feel comfortable. But in order to do that, he basically mimicked what I was saying.

Weeks went by and Larry began to get the hang of Christian prayer. He seemed to be learning the language of it as though he were an insider, albeit stumbling along and, yes, sometimes even by swearing in his prayers. By then the cancer in his lungs had spread to a tumor in his neck that gave him severe pain. Pagitt visited Larry in his home to be with him and to pray. As they talked, they took turns reading important passages to each other: Pagitt from the Bible, and Larry from American Indian and New Age poetry. Larry's pain was so severe that a number of times he collapsed back on his pillow to rest. As the conversation naturally developed, Pagitt asked Larry what he thought about God. Larry spoke of an experience in the Boundary Waters Canoe Area of northern Minnesota some forty-five years earlier where he had "met Jesus." Not sure what to make of that comment, Pagitt read to Larry the story of Jesus healing the cripple whose friends had lowered him through the roof: "And Jesus seeing their faith said to the paralytic, 'Take courage, my son, your sins are forgiven'" (Mark 2:5). Pagitt recalls:

> He had his eyes closed as I read. But when I read about the cripple's friends, his eyes popped open. "Their faith?" he asked.
> "Larry," I said, "I know that you don't have faith right now, but you have some friends that are giving their faith to you and bringing you to Jesus right now." And Larry reached out and grabbed my hands and closed his eyes and said, "Dear Jesus, give me the faith to believe. Give me what I need to have a faith and believe in God." When we got done, he said almost matter-of-factly: "Damnedest thing, the pain is gone!"

But the story was not over. Larry had said that he had "met Jesus" at age eighteen. It turned out that Larry had had something of an Episcopal upbringing, but because he had left the church by the time he was fourteen, his knowledge of the "Jesus" whom he claimed to have met while canoeing lacked substance. Over the course of his life Larry had become an alcoholic and then a recovering alcoholic. Eventually he had drifted toward American Indian and New Age religions. The teachers in his Episcopalian Sunday school had taught him to interpret the story of his earliest spiritual experience in terms of a Jesus figure, but in his later years he thought he could better tell his life story in the language of Alcoholics Anonymous and Indian spiritualism. However, Pagitt observed that over the few months Larry had been linked up with Solomon's Porch, the language Larry spoke was beginning to change again.

The first week of January found Pagitt at Larry's bedside again, this time in the hospital bed at home. Thinking of yet another neck surgery Larry was scheduled to have the following morning, Pagitt asked, "Larry, about what can I pray for you?" Lying in a hospital bed, fitted with a halo neck brace so he can't move his neck (his first surgery was very deep), and looking terrible, Larry responded in a raspy voice, "Naaah, I can't really think of a thing. I'm just so glad that there is a personal God who's gonna love me and care for me all the way through this thing."

Pagitt was astonished! Not only had Larry's stance toward his cancer changed over a few short months, from warfare to serenity, Larry was speaking of God in ways Pagitt had never heard from him. Pagitt explained, "I'd never said anything about a personal God to him. It was in the context of hearing all the conversations around Solomon's Porch—

the worship songs, the Lord's Table, discussions with other believers—
that Larry must have picked up the truth that Christians follow a personal
God."

Pagitt was aware that people like Larry present a unique challenge for
ministry. He mused, "What kind of spiritual development can you do with
a guy dying of cancer? For what purpose is he supposed to grow spiritually? He's not going to be an elder. . . . He's going to die soon." Slowly
and deliberately, Pagitt began to teach Larry the language of resurrection.
"Christians are not people of perpetual life. We are people of resurrection." Thus Pagitt reminds those gathered at Solomon's Porch that
Eucharist is to be taken in anticipation of a new heaven and earth; some-
day it will all be recreated. In the meantime, Pagitt continually revisits
Revelation 21 with them and with Larry: one day there'll no longer be any
pain, weeping, or crying. This pain, Larry's pain—it all goes away. The
cancer? It will be gone. "This new world is what Christians are all about."

Larry is one of the "youngest" believers at Solomon's Porch. But the
way he speaks is powerfully shaping the rest of the community. Pagitt
prepares his sermons in light of conversations with a Tuesday night Bible
discussion group. When the group was studying James 1, finding joy in
your trials, a young college woman raised a question. She has a life-long
disease, not entirely debilitating, but rare enough for her to be on experimental medication that is manufactured in France. Sometimes the supply
is erratic, and when it runs out, she is in significant pain. She asked, "Is
this passage saying that I'm suppose to find joy in all this stuff?" Pagitt,
who had just come from Larry's bedside, recounted the words of a man
dying of cancer, "Naaah, I can't really think of a thing. I'm just so glad
that there is a personal God who's gonna love me and care for me all the
way through this thing." One by one people teared up. As he tells the
story, Pagitt gets a twinkle in his eye:

> It was almost like people at NASA who, having witnessed a successful
> launch, turn to each other and say, half in triumph, half in surprise: "It worked!"
> That's what dawned on us regarding Larry. You see, literally all the stuff
> Christians say is just theory until someone like Larry speaks it. When I
> repeated Larry's words in this context, we were all overcome. "Holy cow! It
> works! We're not just messin' around!"

Larry is dying. By his own admission, among the worst things about his sickness is that he hasn't been able to be at Solomon's Porch for several weeks. Shortly after his latest surgery he was trying to convince Teresa to bring him, wearing his neck brace, to Solomon's Porch: "If we get there about an hour early, I think I can make it up the stairs."

What can we learn about evangelism from Larry's story? In particular, Larry's story helps us to see ways in which conversion involves learning to think in a new language.

We sometimes think we are objective observers of the events that constitute our lives. It seems ridiculous to suggest that something might happen within our purview and we wouldn't immediately know both that something had happened and what it was that happened. But surprisingly, when we lack the right phrase for describing an event, the details tend to escape our notice. "It happened so fast," we say, "it was all a blur." The pace of events, however, is not our only enemy. We actually may be predisposed to overlook details, even to miss the fact that something happened at all, by a set of expectations we unconsciously hold and use to sort out the blur of events that constitute our daily living. When the events of life fail to fit our expectations, our mental processes short-circuit so that we sometimes fail to identify an event correctly; sometimes we fail to identify that it occurred at all!

In a psychological experiment that deserves to be far better known outside the trade, Bruner and Postman asked experimental subjects to identify on short and controlled exposure a series of playing cards. Many of the cards were normal, but some were made anomalous, e.g., a red six of spades and a black four of hearts. Each experimental run was constituted by the display of a single card to a single subject in a series of gradually increased exposures. After each exposure the subject was asked what he had seen, and the run was terminated by two successive correct identifications.

Even on the shortest exposures many of the subjects identified most of the cards, and after a small increase all the subjects identified them all. For the normal cards these identifications were usually correct, but anomalous cards were almost always identified, without apparent hesitation or puzzlement, as normal. The black four of hearts might, for example, be identified as the four of either spades or hearts. Without any awareness of trouble, it was immediately fitted to one of the conceptual categories prepared by prior experience. One would not even like to say that the subjects had seen something different from what they identified. With a further increase of exposure to the anomalous cards, subjects did begin to hesitate and to display awareness of anomaly. Exposed, for example, to the red six of spades, some would say: That's the six of spades, but there's something wrong with it—the black has a red border. Further increase of exposure resulted in still more hesitation until finally, and sometimes quite suddenly, most subjects would produce the correct identification without hesitation. Moreover, after doing this with two or three anomalous cards, they would have little further difficulty with the others. A few subjects, however, were never able to make the requisite adjustments of their categories. Even at forty times the average exposure required to recognize normal cards for what they were, more than 10 percent of the anomalous cards were not correctly identified. And the subjects who then failed often experienced acute personal distress. One of them exclaimed: "I can't make the suit out, whatever it is. It didn't even look like a card that time. I don't know what color it is now or whether it's a spade or a heart. I'm not even sure now what a spade looks like. My God!"[17]

The panic these subjects felt came from their inability to do something simple: identify playing cards. Apparently the identity of simple objects isn't always self-evident. Because the color of some playing cards fell outside the scope of their expectations, some of the subjects couldn't make identification of the red six of spades or the black four of hearts at all. Our awareness of what happens to us is conditioned by our expectations; in some instances at least we only see what we expect to see.

The language we speak is one of the primary factors contributing to our ability to correctly describe the events that make up our lives. It is this fact that prompted theologian George Lindbeck to conclude, "it is necessary to have the means for expressing an experience in order to have it, and the richer our expressive or linguistic system, the more subtle, varied, and differentiated can be our experience."[18] Pediatricians and child psychologists use pictures of human faces in various expressions of pain to help young children identify their level of discomfort, because children are notoriously inept at putting sensation into words. This becomes even more complicated when children try to express their emotions. Their ineptitude may be evidence that they do not feel what an adult would feel in a similar situation. Children may not only misidentify their feelings, but if they lack the requisite vocabulary, they may even lack certain emotions. Even if the physical symptoms, such as heart rate, blood pressure, and galvanic skin response, are similar to those of an adult, can we really say that a child feels, for example, chagrined?

We see this experiential ambiguity played out in Larry's story. When he had an unusual experience as a young adult, his reflex was to describe it in the only terms he had available: he described it as a religious encounter with the Jesus of his Episcopalian Sunday school class. We are inclined to say he was right about the referent of that description, yet because Larry knew so little about this Jesus character, not only was the description not completely convincing, it didn't stick. The experience neither was self-evident nor did it drive him to Christian discipleship. Rather, the event was inherently facile, conformable to a number of competing descriptions. Although Christian observers may feel sure that Larry really did meet Jesus, the only thing we know for certain is that Larry later described his experience as an encounter with the faceless higher power he learned about in his twelve-step program, and then as the immanent force alluded to in popular New Age religion. My point is not to settle which description was correct, but to illustrate that the aptness of our descriptions is always a function of our fluency in a conceptual language.

Although we may think Larry's conversion story is outside the bounds of normalcy, in an age of increasing biblical illiteracy, Larry's case may be becoming more the norm than the exception. Consequently, we see in Larry's case the importance of language acquisition for conversion and thus the need for language training as a component of our evangelism.

When seventeenth-century Puritan Richard Baxter became pastor of a nominally Christian congregation, his strategy to win converts was to institute catechism classes.[19] Baxter traveled from farmhouse to farmhouse on Sunday afternoons teaching plain folk the doctrines of the faith. After a year, revival broke out in his church. According to his account, many formerly nominal Christians became true converts. One way to understand the large number of conversions he observed is that as they received catechesis, parishioners were for the first time becoming fluent in the Christian language. This leads us to another story.

Fluency by Catechesis: Heidi

A girl named Heidi recently dropped off her application to be a summer camp counselor at Colonial (Congregational) Church.[20] She's a sophomore in high school, and the essay on her application began:

> My faith journey has been one of ups and downs. It started off as a down. My first time really learning and loving God was confirmation. Confirmation in my family was important but I didn't know anything about God. I was basically forced to go. I ended up loving it very much. I looked forward to Wednesday nights where I could go and learn more about God. Confirmation was one of the biggest steppingstones in my faith journey. That was what jump-started my love and interest for God. . . . I am really glad my faith journey turned out the way it did. Getting to know and love God has changed my life, views, and beliefs forever.

It is instructive that Heidi marks the beginning of her spiritual journey by a series of classes over which she had very little choice. Every year at Colonial Church, twenty or thirty reluctant kids are dutifully deposited by their parents at church on a Wednesday night in September for confirmation orientation night. Knowing that some of them are present against their will, Pastor Tony Jones does his best to take the sting out of the night. He asks the students, "How many of you really don't want to be here?" About a third of them—the honest ones!—raise their hands. Jones asks them to give confirmation a chance. "Church isn't so boring and history can be really exciting. I promise that you will learn words from different languages, and if you're good, you might even get to borrow the acolyte get-up for Halloween!"

Over the course of the next fourteen months, these high school freshmen learn about the Apostles' Creed and the Lord's Prayer and the Ten Commandments and the sacraments. They learn how to read the Bible and how to pray, and they learn all about the history of the church and the history of Congregationalism and the history of Colonial Church. They learn how the church is governed and how sermons are prepared and how the worship service is put together. And they learn the meaning of words like heresy, invocation, orthodox, and maundy.

Conventional wisdom might say that this is a great way to drive kids away from the church. On the contrary, Jones has found it to be a highly effective outreach tool. Although he works hard to make confirmation fun, interactive, and dialogical, at its core the strength of Colonial Church's confirmation attendance isn't about the programmatic elements. Rather, it is about the power of what the ancients called catechesis. Jones admits that every year a few kids drop out. But in his experience, the dropouts are vastly outnumbered by kids like Heidi for whom God becomes real through confirmation.

As with Larry, the means by which God became real for Heidi was her acquisition of the Christian conceptual language. This skill involves more than mere vocabulary retention; it involves knowing how to go on in a conversation in ways that do not transgress the practical and historical boundaries of terms. In Heidi's case, this language instruction had an added formal dimension. Foreign languages are best learned through a mixture of immersion and instruction, and Heidi's immersion in the life of her church was augmented by the language instruction called catechism.

We shouldn't be surprised by stories like Heidi's or Richard Baxter's congregation's. After all, when the apostle Paul took up the task of preaching to the Gentiles, his strategy was to establish a school in the house of a God-fearer named Titus Justus (Acts 18:7–11). While the Gentiles had the advantage of their openness to the gospel, they had the disadvantage of their relative ignorance of the story's beginning in the Old Testament. Jews who were well-versed in this history had no trouble catching the drift of sermons by Stephen or Peter or Paul. But when Paul was faced with a biblically illiterate audience, he opened a school. He spent a year and a half there, and all the while a steady stream of Corinthians were coming to faith in Christ.

Granted, the text in Acts 18 is syncopated. It doesn't explicitly specify a causal connection between the catechetical instruction in Titus's home and the steady rate of conversions in Corinth, but there is a pattern there that suggests the advice I've been giving. Remember, beliefs come in intradependent sets. One cannot believe in the incarnation without believing in Christ's deity, and one cannot believe in Christ's deity without believing in a plurality within the one God. In this regard, conversion is akin to the shifting of paradigms. In the heyday of evangelicalism (during the 1950s in America), the paradigm shift the evangelist sought was minimally disruptive for the listener because most Americans held nominally orthodox beliefs about the identity of God, the authority of Scripture, the life of Jesus as morally normative, and so on. That is no longer the case. People seem more likely to believe in the ubiquity of wraiths than in the deity of Christ! A typical nonbeliever who is invited to embrace Jesus today must make a wholesale trade of an enormous web of beliefs for those of Christian orthodoxy. An evangelist can assist a friend's paradigm shift by sharing enough of the implications of Jesus' story—when this sharing is systematized, we call the presentation catechesis—to render plausible the friend's wager on the coherence of the Christian web of beliefs.

This is quite different from giving would-be converts a course in Christian apologetics. What is most useful for their conversion are not explanations of tough questions that can supposedly be understood by anyone regardless of their theological literacy or relative indifference to the Savior. Rather, what is needed is the sort of guidance Philip gave the Ethiopian eunuch in Acts 8. St. Jerome explains that even though the eunuch

> was holding a book in his hand and was reflecting on the words of the Lord, even sounding them with his tongue and pronouncing them with his lips, . . . he did not know who he was worshipping in this book. Then Philip came, and showed him Jesus hidden in the letter. . . . What a marvelous teacher![21]

My point is that by revealing Jesus "hidden in the letter," Philip acted more as an art instructor than as a high school history teacher. The eunuch didn't need to memorize names and dates; he needed to see the pattern embedded in the text. So Philip retold the story, expanding the context and assisting the eunuch in making the connections between Isaiah's story and the recent events in Jerusalem. The resulting knowledge was more than mere information. It was what Michael Polanyi calls "personal knowledge" because it could not be understood apart from the realization of the claim that the knowing laid upon the knower's life.[22] The eunuch was baptized, expressing his solidarity with the Jerusalem church despite his geographic separation from it.

Of course, because the eunuch was likely of Jewish descent (note his possession of the Old Testament Scriptures), it makes sense to expect a rapid conversion on his part. Augustine's conversion took much longer. Perhaps conversion stories like Augustine's are the reason catechism in the early days of the church could last up to three years.

Unfortunately, the crucial role this type of instruction has for the conversion of postmodern nonbelievers requires that the church be filled with experienced guides. As Lindbeck puts it, "just as an individual becomes human by learning a language, so he or she becomes a new creature through hearing and interiorizing the language that speaks of Christ."[23] Bland sermons about universal love and other theological niceties will not do the trick. What is needed is concrete familiarity with the nitty-gritty of the biblical stories. And as we saw earlier, Lindbeck is not at all optimistic that today's churches have preserved the Christian language well enough to train the next generation to speak fluently. A church needs more than seeker-sensitivity and user-friendliness to pass on a language as old and rich as that of Christianity.[24] But this is precisely what Baxter's classes supplied his parishioners.

Catechism is one easily overlooked resource for increasing the skill that would-be Christ-followers need to recognize the pattern of Jesus' story. But there are other, less systematic means for learning the Christian language. Language does not consist of putting verbal labels on private mental images. If it did, language learning would be merely memorizing vocabulary. Rather, language is proactive. Language use goes proxy for other behaviors. Consequently, language can only be learned by participation.

When a toddler skins her knee, she involuntarily cries. Although she may not consciously intend her crying as a form of communication, her reflex serves that purpose. A slightly older child may run all the way home without shedding a tear, but once in the door, within sight of Mom, burst into tears. In turn, the child's pain behavior triggers a reflex from her mother. After observing the atypical behavior (for the child is not given to crying without good reason) and assessing the damage to the skinned knee, does the mother reassure the child by explaining that the abrasion resulted from the sidewalk's high coefficient of friction? Of course not! The mother does not infer from the child's behavior that the child is in pain. Rather, her reflex is automatic. Without thinking, she scoops the child into her arms and coos, "There, there, I know it hurts."

In one sense, the reflex of crying does not express private pain; it is a social behavior that gains for us reassurance from others that we are not alone. Imagine the terror we would feel if others responded with complete indifference to our groans of pain! This is why "weeping with those who weep" is more appropriate than offering explanation to those who suffer. In the interaction between a mother and child, the child begins to associate the phrase "it hurts" (first spoken by the mother) with the behavior of crying. When the child is an adult, she may once again skin her knee, but then the words "Wow, does that ever hurt!" replace the crying.

So then, learning a language is not memorizing a vocabulary. Rather, it is learning new behaviors that go proxy for other behaviors. We learn to say "ouch" in place of crying when we skin our knee. But the statement of pain weaves us into the lives of others, for speech is the fabric of community life. Moreover, speaking is not simply the exchange of words with others. Our words only have meaning insofar as we are engaged in doings. At its core, learning a language involves a whole new way of behaving. As one philosopher put it, the grammar of the word *book* is bound up not so much with the objects we call books, but with the activities we do with them. Only those who fetch books, stack books, count books, read books, and so on become fluent in the use of the word. In like fashion, becoming a Christ-follower means gaining fluency in the language of Christ. This is no simple phrase-by-phrase same-saying. Rather, fluency involves engagement in an entirely different form of living with others. Outside of this there is no salvation.

The changed lives of Doreen, Larry, and Heidi are real. At some points their stories are so striking that we rightly shake our heads in amazement and conclude that God must be at work. On the assumption that these conversions are genuine, we do well to pay attention to just in what manner God's Spirit is at work, to see what we can learn for the practice of evangelism. To this end postmodern categories help us see what we might have otherwise overlooked. Doreen's story helps us see that conversion takes time. It takes time because conversion involves becoming socially embedded in the community of faithful Christ-followers. Part and parcel of becoming an insider is the learning of the Christian conceptual language. Acquisition of fluency is itself a time-intensive task. Larry's story helps us see that fluency is gained by immersion, which is to say, by living in close proximity to native speakers who engage the novice in conversations conducted in the host language. Heidi's story helps us see that fluency may be improved when immersion is accompanied by formal language instruction called catechesis. The catechesis advocated here however is not the bland and dusty vocabulary-by-rote approach. Rather, postmodern insights about the permeation of language and world underscore the common sense advice that catechesis must involve a high degree of hands-on activity.

The role of participation brings us to the final two stories. In them we will discover the power of narrative for evangelism.

5

Living the Story

Language permeates the world. We learn what words mean as they go proxy for certain behaviors. We learn the significance of behaviors when they are explained to us by means of words. These two threads come together powerfully in what has been called the narrative texture of human life.

In the last chapter we saw how the Christian conceptual language could be learned by a combination of immersion into the life of the believing community and by formal instruction of catechesis. This present chapter looks further at the nature of the community into which the would-be convert is to be immersed. What makes a community "Christian" isn't simply the fact that all the members hold roughly the same beliefs, but that they live out those beliefs with each other in ways that are faithful to the story of Jesus. The christoform pattern of these lived-out beliefs is what constitutes their "form of life."

In the last chapter we met Larry who absorbed the idea that
God was personal simply through regular contact with other
believers. In this chapter we first meet Allen who becomes per-
suaded to embrace Christ by direct involvement in a community that is imitating Christ's care for the poor and dispossessed
(Luke 4:18–19; 6:20–21). By his engagement in this ministry *as
a practitioner*, Allen tried on the Christian form of life and discovered a perfect fit. In the second scenario, we will meet a
church that taps into the aesthetic power of narrative for doing
evangelism.

Form of Life: Allen

Allen is a very intelligent young man, a writer for the local newspaper.[1] He met Pastor Brad Cecil about two years ago for lunch. He
claimed himself to be an atheist because he had some serious questions
about the reliability of Christianity:

> In my junior year of high school, I developed some problems with who God
> was. I didn't think it was right for wars to happen, or babies to be born with
> AIDS, or for people to starve for lack of food. If God was a God of love then
> he wouldn't allow such things to occur, because nothing in the lives of peo-
> ple deserved that kind of pain and suffering.

These troubles haunted Allen throughout college. He spent countless
hours surfing from Internet site to Internet site reading whatever he
could, sometimes going days without sleep. And the more he read, the
more convinced he had become that God couldn't exist.

Pastor Cecil admitted to him that there was something essentially
unsatisfying with all so-called answers to the sorts of challenging questions that Allen raised. So he refrained from trying to answer them.
Rather, Cecil offered Allen a chance to experience genuine Christianity,
to see up close what it was all about.

Allen was intrigued by Cecil's proposal. Over the next six months,
Allen was a regular at Axxess Church worship services. He had moved
to Texas from his home state of Idaho during his third year of college. As
a journalism major he had landed a part-time job at the Dallas Morning
News. He was also working at a local eatery, where he met Rachel, who

invited him to tag along while she fulfilled a college course requirement by participating in a "poverty simulation weekend." Allen expected that the weekend would be filled with talk about social issues. What he got was a weekend living without money. That weekend brought Allen face to face with the message of the gospel in Matthew 25: Those who fed, clothed, visited, and cared for the "least of these" were those who fed, clothed, visited, and cared for Jesus himself. Allen recalls the crisis this precipitated for him: "The poverty simulation was an awakening for me. I was able to experience who Christ was, I was able to see the face of our Lord, and it allowed me knowledge that I had either ignored or just hadn't seen before."

After that weekend, Allen began regularly volunteering his time in compassion ministry to local poor people.

Six months passed.

> The weeks that followed that weekend were ones of turmoil for me. My world had just been shattered, and I was trying to piece together what it was that I had known. This went on for several weeks, until one night, during a meteor shower, God and I had a talk (mostly one-sided on my part). Watching the lights streak across the sky, I noticed four stars to the left of Orion (the constellation) that formed a near perfect cross. It amazed me that I would notice something such as that at a time in which I was going through what I was going through. At that point I realized the existence of God.

As was the custom, Brad Cecil's church served communion at midnight on Christmas Eve. Allen came forward to receive communion with tears streaming down his face. He had been at communion services at the church before but had never partaken, reminding Cecil that he was an atheist. Hoping that Allen's decision this time wasn't simply due to the sentimentality of the occasion, before Cecil administered communion to him, he asked Allen whether something about his atheism had changed. Allen's yes was very convincing, and for the first time Allen took communion as a self-proclaimed follower of Jesus.

When they met later to talk, Cecil asked Allen to explain his change of heart. Allen said he wasn't sure what it was exactly, but something was happening to him. It had started on the poverty simulation weekend and had grown throughout his involvement with other Christ-followers in serving local poor people and worshiping together. Gradually his stance had begun to change despite the fact that he had never received satisfactory answers to his questions. Apparently, his experience with the community of Christ had trumped the questions.

As Cecil notes, observers of Allen's change can't pinpoint a time when his conversion happened. On the contrary, his conversion seemed to be a gradual process, longer than any that Cecil had ever observed. Allen claims that his conversion is still happening. His participation in the language and activities of the believing community clearly played a much more significant role in his transformation than any quantity of apologetics could have accomplished. In spite of the fact that he still doesn't have answers to his questions, Allen is actively moving toward leadership in the community and has expressed a desire to pursue a career of ministry.

Like those of Doreen and Larry, Allen's conversion has taken time—two years and still running. But Allen's story is even more striking for the way hands-on participation in the Christian form of life—in this case, the poverty simulation weekend—was instrumental in his coming to faith. Why should this be?

A common feature in the modern approach to theology is its assumption that propositional knowledge is crucial to faith. Of course, the ultimate object of faith is God, and the seat of saving faith is the regenerate will. However, conservative theologians in the modern period emphasized that faith is hamstrung by ignorance of biblical propositions. Thus American theologian Louis Berkhof wrote in the middle of the last century that "the knowledge of faith consists in a positive recognition of the truth, in which man accepts as true whatsoever God says in His Word."[2] Here Berkhof stands shoulder to shoulder with the Reformers in rejecting the notion of implicit faith (*fides implicita*) because faith without propositional content is not faith at all.[3] The claim that conversion is an informed process is correct, as far as it goes. What modern thinkers have trouble explaining is the fact that we are rarely moved to faith by either simple proof texts or carefully crafted apologetic answers. One of the troubles is that apologetic answers often fall on ears that appear to be stone deaf. We often forget how much must already be in place for answers, whether spoken or written, to even be understood, much less believed. A number of different conditions must be met in order for Christian language to hit its mark. Once we see the close connection between speech acts, actions that we take with words, and nonlinguistic acts, we will be able to appreciate that Allen's journey toward faith, despite the lack of apologetics answers, was not uninformed after all.

First, in order for Christian language to hit its mark, one must know the linguistic conventions by which we communicate. Imagine how bewildered one might feel to face for the first time a sentence such as:

Τῇ γὰρ χάριτί ἐστε σεσωσμένοι διὰ; πίστεως

Only someone fluent in Koine Greek will recognize the sentence as Ephesians 2:8 "For by grace you have been saved through faith" (NRSV). The requirement that one must know the linguistic conventions of a sentence in order to understand it is sometimes lost on us because we frame theological sentences in English for other speakers of English. But we must be careful not to overlook a special conceptual language, complete with its own linguistic conventions, hiding within the English we speak. For example, Christians believe in a trinitarian God, but we cannot properly refer to the Trinity as a "them." Speaking rightly of the plurality within God must stop short of anything that might be construed as tritheism. That is a hidden rule according to which Christians have been trained to speak. When a hidden rule is broken, it sounds bad to the orthodox believer, but the infraction may be more serious than a simple offense to theological grammarians. When these hidden rules are entirely disregarded, the Christian speaker will be as unintelligible as the dinner guest who blurts, "Justice chair sunrise!"[4]

Second, the identity of a proposition's author may alter the proposition's sense. For example, we might be asked whether the following sentence is true or false: "What separates two people most profoundly is a different sense of cleanliness." When we hesitate to answer, we may be prodded: "Either a sentence is true or it is false—so which is it?" But that isn't playing fair. As it stands, the sentence is ambiguous. One might imagine such a claim being made by an obsessively spic and span housewife of the 1940s who ranked children's moral character by their tidiness. Perhaps a Reformer such as Martin Luther had *spiritual* cleanliness in mind and spoke the sentence as a plea that our righteousness exceed that of the scribes and Pharisees. In point of fact, the claim was made by Friedrich Nietzsche, who dismissed moral and spiritual properties as fantasy. Clearly, the supposed plain sense of the text is governed by the identity of the one who speaks it.

Third, the context within which a sentence is spoken alters the meaning it conveys. During the German invasion of France, a French commander explained that France needed six strong lines of defense because "France is hexagonal." Think of such a sentence spoken instead at a conference of cartographers. A mapmaker who claimed France was hexagonal wouldn't sell many maps, and rightly so, for we expect more guidance from our maps than a hexagon can supply. But in a war room, such a simplistic sentence makes sense. (On the other hand, considering what happened to France in the Second World War, perhaps the sentence is false after all.) One must be at least as familiar with the context in which a sentence is spoken as one is with its vocabulary in order to understand it.

The fourth way that our understanding of language hinges on extralinguistic factors can be seen in the example of shoes. Children learn to speak at about the same time they learn to walk. Of course, children prefer to tool around on bare tip-toes, and the wrestling match that is mistaken for getting a young child dressed isn't over until shoes are found, matched, wedged on (don't forget to straighten the child's toes), laced, tied, and double-tied. All the while, the parent is talking "Now then, where are your shoe— . . . Ah! Here they are. Let's put on your . . . sit still, please!, while we finish putting on your shoes." And still some children manage to kick off their shoes before they even get down the hallway! Moving at full speed through a room scattered with Legos, the barefoot child winces with surprise and screams out in pain. After rushing to the rescue, the parent soothes the child with a word spoken with great tenderness: "shoes." Slowly the child begins to associate the word *shoe* with a variety of activities. Shoes are for wearing, throwing, dropping, losing, kicking off, finding, lacing, unlacing, mismatching, knotting, double-tying, and so forth. Apart from these activities, the word *shoe* has no meaning.

In the hurly-burly of each day, the child begins to pair the word *shoe* with all the activities associated with shoes. Thus sentences that include the word *shoe* comes to have sense for the child because of the activities. Without such activities, the word *shoe* would remain as enigmatic for the child as the word "enigma." It might even make sense to say that such activities imprint the child with the sense of the word *shoe*.

If words for simple objects such as shoes are learned by their proximity to certain activities, then the basis of our fluency in a language is engagement in these activities. While wearing shoes is a simple activity that makes sense for its own sake, some activities are more closely tied with complex behaviors that only make sense when juxtaposed with a community's form of life.

Thus, the fifth way that linguistic fluency is a function of non-linguistic behavior is the way it requires participation in those activities that constitute the distinctive identity of a particular community. For example, consider the analogy that Christians see between being physically lost and being spiritually lost.

It was very dark by the time I finished jogging. About a half-mile from home a kindly elderly woman toting a grocery bag flagged me down and asked me how to get to D Street.

"It's about four blocks that way," I said, pointing west.

"Can I get there by going this way?" she inquired, pointing east!

I gently engaged her in conversation and began to walk her home. She told me all about her family back in Pennsylvania; how her husband, now passed on, had worked for the film industry; how many years she had lived in San Bernardino; how she was Catholic and went to Mass every week at Our Lady of Assumption; how she had two darling nieces who loved to talk on the phone to Auntie.

"Well, here we are on D Street." I said at last. "Which house is yours?"

She looked at me uncomprehendingly. After an uncomfortable pause I asked her for her house number.

"3587 D Street," she responded instantly. That was only two houses away.

"That's this way."

"OK," she replied and followed obediently. Along the way she recounted the names of neighbors whose houses she did not recognize. "Then this must be Mrs. Peterson's. And across the street would be Dr. Lopez. He's retired now, but such a nice man."

When we were in front of her house, the first house she recognized, she remarked, "Well, I'll never do that again!" She had only intended to walk to the grocery store for a Duraflame log for her fireplace. Somehow, in walking home, she had gotten all turned around. I listened in horror as she said that next time she would be sure to take the car.

I encouraged her not to venture out again, especially so close to dark, without one of her friends for company. I waited while she fished her keys out of her purse and got safely into her house.

As I retraced my steps toward home I was stunned by what had taken place. Had she taken her car, she would have ended up in Arizona. Had I not stopped to help her she could have easily crossed paths with some local ruffians or worse. But what I found most disconcerting was how totally unconcerned she seemed to be and how completely unaware she was of her plight.

Christians see a resemblance between nonbelievers and this woman: not merely lost, but completely lost, headed in the wrong direction and both unaware and unconcerned. But how can this be? When the stakes are so high—eternal, in fact—how can nonbelievers be unaware of their plight? Conversely, why does it so rarely cross our minds to wonder whether we may be lost? Of course we happily admit "once I was lost, but now am found." Yet we do not apply the notion of spiritual lostness to ourselves in the same way we apply it to others. That change in application is part of the grammar of lostness and constitutes Christian belief. I submit that nonbelievers simply stand outside the form of life that both marks us as Christian believers and school us in the language of lostness. Who are we? We are those who pray for the lost, sing about the plight of the lost, give thanks that we are no longer lost, heed sermons about our responsibility to the lost, and bear witness to the lost. Just what kind of Christians would we be if we never prayed, sang, thanked, heeded, or witnessed? The degree to which we engage in all these activities is the degree to which we naturally apply the analogy of physical lostness to others' spiritual condition. Conversely, nonbelievers who stand outside all such activities do not even have the category "lost" in their treasury of self-descriptions. Consequently, the question "Am I lost?" never occurs to them. How could it, so long as *spiritual* lostness makes about as much sense to them as the nonsensical *bleen* lostness. We've been looking at conditions under which speakers are able to gain fluency in a conceptual language so we can expand our notion of conversion from *assent to a set of propositions* to *fluency that engages one in a form of life*. For the five reasons I've discussed, propositions alone—whether the sentences of apologetic answers, or statements of faith, or even verses from the Bible—are insufficient to compel understanding. Uptake requires mastery of grammatical conventions, knowledge of speaker and context, familiarity with activities, and participation in a community's distinctive form of life. Last of all, the quality of listeners' understanding is a function of their knowledge of history.

One day in early seventeenth-century Holland, an Anabaptist farmer and his little boy were crossing a narrow bridge with a wagon filled with hay when they met coming toward them a Calvinist farmer also driving a team of horses pulling a fully loaded wagon. Being first on the bridge, the Anabaptist farmer said, "Please back your wagon off the bridge so that I might pass."

Being very much in a hurry and unwilling to fiddle with unhitching and rehitching his team, the Calvinist replied, "See here, please back *your* wagon off the bridge that *I* might pass."

The debate continued several minutes until the Anabaptist farmer stood up and removed his coat, which until now had concealed his bulging muscles, and said simply, "If you do not back up your wagon, then I am going to do something that I will very much regret later!"

Hastily, the Calvinist farmer complied. As they journeyed on, the Anabaptist's little boy—whose eyes were as saucers—inquired timidly, "Papa, Papa! What were you going to do?" The Anabaptist farmer replied honestly, "What can I say? I would have backed up my wagon."

This story is humorous because Anabaptists are known for their longtime commitment to pacifism. They are little talked about in the annals of history because they cannot boast of a single military victory. Surely this unbroken record shapes how an Anabaptist community instinctively hears "Vengeance is mine, I will repay, says the Lord" (Rom. 12:19 NRSV): "We must not fight. For fighting, if it is to be done at all, is God's job, not ours."

The message Calvinists have gleaned from Romans 12:19 is quite different. The Calvinist reasons that if a war satisfies certain just-war criteria, then it is their duty, as God's stewards of creation and culture, to fight such a war for the honor and will of God. In fact, the possibility of engaging in violence is precisely what schools the Calvinist farmer to take the removal of a coat as a threat. This outlook also gives Calvinists a certain resoluteness in their conception of duty. As one seventeenth-century observer of the religious wars remarked, "I had rather see coming toward me a whole regiment with drawn swords, than one lone Calvinist [convinced] that he is doing the will of God!"[5] My point is simply this, the communities to which Anabaptists and Calvinists belong train them to understand Romans 12:19 in the ways they do.

Because there are preconditions to our understanding, the knowledge that we require for conversion is tacit,[6] coming not by way of apologetic answers to tough questions but by way of formation, the forming of our lives by mastery of grammatical conventions, knowledge of the speaker, comprehension of context, familiarity with relevant activities, participation in a community's form of life, and imaginative reliving of the community's history. Someone who achieves all six of these preconditions has the possibility of understanding the apologetic answers. However, and somewhat surprisingly, once these preconditions are in place, apologetics is often no longer required. There is a sense in which participation in the form of life of a community trumps the questions one might initially bring. In other words, one doesn't move from apologetic answers to faith because the adoption of the form of life prerequisite to understanding the answers is the very conversion aimed at in the first place.

Returning to the story of Allen, we can see why his participation in a particular form of life contributed to a shift in his beliefs. In the first place, Allen's conversion began with his close proximity to Christian worship. Although he was a spectator, Allen gained imaginative ability to envision being an insider once he had been invited inside the bounds of the believing community.[7] Good anthropologists know what this means. To understand a culture well and to speak fairly on its behalf, anthropologists must get close enough to envision what being an insider is like. Thus Peter Winch spoke of the categorical mistake that technocentric cultures made when evaluating so-called primitive societies.[8] Westerners are apt to label preliterate cultures backward on the assumption that aborigines will abandon their superstitions once they learn, for example, that meteorology is superior to rain dances when it comes to predicting the weather. Ironically, these cultures may indeed adopt Western technology and yet not abandon their former practices. Why not? Well, anthropologists who are close enough explain that dancing functions neither as a predictor nor controller of the future.[9] *That* mistaken conclusion was made by people too far away to appreciate the "primitive" culture as a rival of Western culture, a rival that does *not* assume that prediction and control are the ultimate human goods.

Just as outsiders to the preliterate culture will draw wrong conclusions about its practices, but anthropologists are in a better position than Western laypeople to draw proper conclusions, so too Allen's proximity to authentic worship—one of the constitutive practices of the church[10]—gives him the vantage point for imaginatively inhabiting the Christian outlook, even to the point of beginning to empathize with the motivation behind Christian speech and practice.

The second moment of Allen's conversion was his involvement in the poverty simulation weekend. We in the West, who comprise only 5 percent of the world's population but consume 23 percent of its energy, sometimes overlook the centrality of economics for Jesus' kingdom. Jesus addresses the topic of wealth and poverty more frequently than he does heaven, hell, sexual immorality, or violence. In fact, one out of every ten verses in the Synoptic Gospels contains direct teaching on economic issues.[11] Despite that which some find objectionable in liberation theology, we must concede that the liberation theologians have done us a great service by yanking our attention back to the New Testament's central economic agenda. There is a clear connection between the plight of the poor and dispossessed and Jesus' perception of his own identity as the Messiah who has come to

bring good news to the poor. . . .
to proclaim release to the captives
and recovery of sight to the blind
to let the oppressed go free
to proclaim the year of the Lord's favor (Luke 4:18-20 NRSV).

What is my point? Simply this: the solidarity Allen was forced to share with the poor that weekend helped school his imagination, in a way not otherwise possible, to see the plight of the powerless as a first step in seeing his own.

Allen's exercise wasn't the first time that role-playing poverty led to spiritual conversion. In the thirteenth century, young Francis, an aristocrat from Assisi, paused in front of the opulent St. Peter's church barely long enough to exchange garments with a beggar and take his place on the dirty streets. The moment when St. Francis (who is commonly regarded as the most Christlike figure in history, save perhaps for Mother Theresa) took the beggar's place in defiance of the wealth of the medieval church was definitive for his conversion. So too for Allen. The poverty simulation weekend forced Allen to see with the eyes of those who inhabit the only economic class that Jesus called "blessed" (Luke 6:20).

In the third moment of his conversion, Allen found himself taking his place among those who are being the hands and feet of Jesus through their service to the local poor. By imitating Jesus, Allen took the stance of a believer, even if he could not yet specify precisely what he was doing. Adopting such a stance is persuasive in and of itself. This fact can even help criminals, such as "Bob" in the story below, learn to pray.

One Thanksgiving weekend the doorbell rang. The young man on the doorstep was dirty, disheveled, smelly, hungry, and wanted by the police. And I knew him! His parents were pillars of the church. He was a straight-A college student, a Phi Beta Kappa, who had once attended a Bible study in my home. I invited him in. As we talked, his story unfolded. "Bob" was no stranger to Christianity. He had, after all, been to Southeast Asia on a missions trip where for the first time he saw what real suffering was like. Sadly, when he began to ask questions about the goodness of God in the face of evils on the street, his church friends tried to get him "saved," thinking that only a non-Christian would ask the sorts of questions he was asking. Not surprisingly, Bob stopped attending church. Instead, he enrolled in secular philosophy courses at the university. He began taking methamphetamines to help his concentration, and sold it to help finance his own habit. Eventually, he became an expert at "taxing," stealing cars for drug lords, and thus became wanted by the police on at least one count (of several hundred possible!) of auto theft.[12] A few weeks later, Bob was caught aiding and abetting a novice car thief and consequently did several months in jail. Although he knew he wanted whatever spiritual reality my family shared, because his conscience was badly seared, he could not bring himself to pray. His conviction of the reality of God was next to nonexistent. Along the way, Bob even tried to commit suicide.

Yet the end of the story is a happy one. Bob is reunited with his family and his church, married to a wonderful believer, the proud father of two lovely girls, a college graduate, and a Certified Managerial Accountant employed by his in-laws' steel industry. I cannot begin to untangle the details of all that led to the completion of Bob's conversion. But let me highlight one of the initial steps.

While Bob was first imprisoned, I secured a Bible for him and urged him to promise to begin reading the Psalms aloud. Because he could not envision God existing, much less listening to him pray, I told him just to pretend that he was the Psalmist and to use the lyrics of each poem as his own. This Bob did. Slowly, he became willing to entertain the notion that perhaps God existed. Bob was pretending to pray. While he was unsure of the reality of the object to whom he prayed, he was not unsure of the stance he was taking by praying. In order even to make-believe he was praying, he had to adopt a certain stance, that of an inferior creature in the presence of a superior Being. This stance seems to have lowered the barrier to further steps Bob made toward his present conviction about the reality of God and his own undeniable dependence upon him.[13]

As is evident in the cases of both Bob and of Allen, involvement in Christian practices—whether praying aloud or serving soup to the poor—carries with it a persuasiveness of its own. Such participation sensitizes people to see what they could not see before. Not only did Allen see the face of Christ in those he served, he also saw the cross of Christ in the constellation of the warrior Orion! The magnitude of this persuasiveness can be heard echoed in the advice of our Christian forebears. In the seventeenth century Blaise Pascal gave sage advice to those who struggled with doubt:

> You would like to attain faith, and do not know the way; you would like to cure yourself of unbelief and ask the remedy for it. Learn of those who have been bound like you, and are cured of an ill of which you would be cured. Follow the way by which they began; by acting, as if they believed, taking the holy water, having masses said.[14]

Likewise, Athanasius advised in the fourth century,

> For the searching and the right understanding of the Scriptures there is need of a good life and pure soul, . . . One cannot possibly understand the teaching of the saints unless one has a pure mind and is trying to imitate their life. . . . Similarly, anyone who wishes to understand the mind of the sacred writers must first cleanse his own life, and approach the saints by copying their deeds.[15]

My point in citing these texts is not to begin a squabble about holy water or the Roman Mass. Rather, our Christian brothers and sisters in the past seemed more aware than we are that our own actions speak louder to us than others' words. As evangelists to a postmodern generation, we would do well to engage others in Christian action as a means of persuasion for Christian truth.

This advice is underscored by the next story. Although participants in the Jesus Freakend were engaged in activity, in this case the activity was not engagement in distinctive Christian practices such as prayer or works of mercy. Rather, they were engaged in recreating the plotline of salvation's story. Their aesthetic participation in the gospel narrative schooled their imagination to more easily apprehend themselves as fallen, diseased, marginalized, in need of rescue, and Jesus as their rescuer.

Storied Imagination: The Jesus Freakend

The Jesus Freakend is a weekend-long experiment in experiential storytelling.[16] The premise is that putting people into the story helps them appreciate the narrative more deeply; it gives the narrative a greater grip on them so that they begin to experience the story as their own. There are no three-point messages on the retreat, no how-tos on Christian living. Rather, participants are urged to trust the Holy Spirit who is present to instruct them as they live out the gospel story. The weekend is made up of four "journeys" and three "meals."

Journey 1—an experience of the story of creation, the fall of humanity, the despair of the intertestamental period, and the powerful joy of Christ's coming, using light, dark, and narration. The light in all of the journeys is from a single candle that is lit when God is tangibly present among people and unlit when he is not. The purpose of this first journey is for participants to better understand the creation story, how sin drove a wedge between God and humanity, and that Jesus was the only way to bring light back to a dark earth.

Journey 2—Participants are told that a gifted orator who speaks for God has come to share with them. The only teaching of the weekend is the complete recitation of the Sermon on the Mount, given by this "Christ figure." This journey enables the participants to hear the unedited and unanalyzed words of Jesus as if they were curious bystanders when the Teacher passed through Galilee.

Parable Stew—Participants are broken up into groups and given the assignment of creating a living parable from one of Christ's teachings. This exercise helps people understand and appreciate Christ's primary form of instruction.

The Bowl of Affliction—Participants are told that there has been a virus running unchecked through the camp and that it affects people in various ways. Some become blind, others lose use of a limb, while others become socially unclean and must wear a sign and stay a certain distance away from everyone else. The only way they can become free is if they can corroborate sightings of a man in a red cloak who has the power to reverse the virus. The purpose of this exercise is to imaginatively experience what it may have felt like to be an outcast physically seeking for the rumored healer from Nazareth.

The Last Supper—The group leaders wash the participants' feet
and serve them a meal. During the meal the Christ figure has
them drink their wine and receive their bread together in
remembrance of him. Each group is then led into the journey
room for the next journey and asked to meditate on sin in their
lives. This exercise powerfully drives home Christ's servant-
hood and the paradox of the Last Supper.

Journey 3—Participants celebrate a short review of the experiences and insights of the previous few days. But they are also
given a foreshadowing of the tragedy to come. A short video of
the crucifixion scene again plunges the journey room into darkness while disturbing and reflective music plays in the background. The intent of this journey is to convey the pain of the
crucifixion necessitated by the despair and darkness of sin.
(Other experiences can be added here, such as the use of
props, music, art, and calligraphy to recreate the stations of the
cross.)

Journey 4 (the next morning)—Light is restored with a short narration and music that captures the incredible mystery and wonder of the resurrection. The participants' candles are then lit
from the single Jesus candle in order to help them experience
the joy of the resurrection and to see light now being made
available to everyone.

Kathy is a young woman who had been instructed about Jesus but
had little idea of who he was. Since attending the Jesus Freakend, she
has given her life over to Christ. She said that she never really knew that
there was such a story, and now she feels completely connected to it.
She suddenly realized that her lifestyle had kept her in darkness and that
it was her sin that had sent Christ to his death. She is now growing in her
faith and slowly purging the bad habits she had formed over a lifetime of
being away from God. The freedom she has found in Christ is difficult for
her to express apart from poetry.

Look here, child, tell me what you see.
I see a star, shining in the sky I see an army of light, caroling the glory I see
a baby in the hay I see the King of the World

Look there, child, now what do you see?
I see footprints in the water I see bread and fish to spare I see eyes that
    now see and ears that now hear I see dead that now walk and demons
    that flee I see a vine, a mustard seed, a lost sheep, a lost son
Open your eyes, child, and what do you see?
I see the Son of David I see the Son of Man I see the Messiah and the Sav-
    ior I see the Hope of the World
Look through my eyes, child, and tell me what you see.
I see a spear and a scourge I see nails and a tree I see the King crowned
    with thorns I see His chest heave and be still I see the Promise fulfilled
    Through the darkness, I see the Light
Help me to show what I see to the world Help me to lead, to witness, to love
I was blind but I see I was deaf but I hear I was dead but now live In You,
    there is life.

The impact of the Jesus Freakend on Kathy illustrates the human heart's need for a particular sort of therapy in order for the light of the gospel to dawn. As Augustine said, the heart is so dark that it must be illumined by God's Spirit if we are to have any hope of perceiving the truth. Yet, as Calvin pointed out, God's Spirit doesn't very often work immediately. Rather, the Spirit is pleased to use other means to accomplish the work of illumination. One means God might use is a human guide. Reflecting on Philip's role in the illumination of the eunuch (Acts 8), St. Jerome rightly concluded: "you cannot advance in the Holy Scriptures unless you have an experienced guide to show you the way."[17] More often than not, such a guide bears a greater resemblance to an art appreciation teacher than to a reference librarian. If I wanted to convince you that Caravaggio is the greatest painter, I could not do it by lecturing on the criteria of great art and then citing the ways Caravaggio meets these criteria, for what prevents you from rejecting the criteria? What I would need to do instead is to help you cultivate a taste for Caravaggio and an eye for great art. That would take hours of guided tours to view actual Caravaggio paintings, tracing shapes and highlighting color schemes, recounting history, and pointing out motifs. In the end, I may only persuade you to prefer Caravaggio to VanGogh, but in this I would have achieved a minor victory, because you would now use Caravaggio's work as a baseline for judging other paintings.

Remember the psychiatric patient, my friend Frank, who read the beginning of Luke's Gospel and perceived Jesus to be a Machiavellian leader? He misunderstood Luke so badly because he was unfamiliar with the terrain of the Scriptures. As a result he misread the landmarks and easily became lost. Like an art student, what he needed was a guided tour. But what means might a tour guide employ?

The specific means that Calvin had in mind were the Word of God and the sacraments of baptism and the Lord's Supper. Some people are fond of quoting Isaiah 55:11, "my word that goes out from my mouth . . . will not return to me empty" (NIV), as if the *words* of the text (perhaps even the letters that make up the words) are a talisman to ward off the evil that might otherwise thwart the divine intention. Such well-meaning persons deliberately lace every conversation with Bible verses in the smug confidence that, sooner or later, the verses will work their magic and penetrate their neighbor's thick heart.

But Calvin had a much richer way of approaching the Scriptures than simply using the biblical text as an incantation or charm.

> For as the aged, or those whose sight is defective, when any book however fair, is set before them, though they perceive that there is something written, are scarcely able to make out two consecutive words, but, when aided by glasses, begin to read distinctly, so Scripture, gathering together the impressions of Deity, which, till then, lay confused in our minds, dissipates the darkness, and shows us the true God clearly.[18]

Calvin's view is quite different from most contemporary approaches to Scripture and is worthy of a closer look. If conservatives err by using Scripture as magic, liberals err by not taking the power of the Scripture seriously enough. Yet since the Enlightenment, liberals and conservatives share the view that Scripture is something to be looked at.[19] The rapid growth of the historical-critical method in the nineteenth century was an extension of the Enlightenment quest for objectivity. In Immanuel Kant's words, enlightenment is

> man's release from his self-incurred tutelage. Tutelage is man's inability to make use of his understanding without direction from

another. Self-incurred is this tutelage when its cause lies not in lack of reason but in lack of resolution and courage to use it without direction from another. *Sapere aude!* "Have courage to use your own reason!"—that is the motto of enlightenment.[20]

In other words, it became widely assumed that the truth of any matter could be gotten at by any mind unfettered by biases and prejudices, especially religious ones. But Calvin would have puzzled over Kant's words. If we shrug off our tutelage, do we not remain untutored? And does not an untutored mind produce an outlook that is lopsided—perhaps as lopsided as the meal foraged by a toddler turned loose on a smorgasbord?

In Calvin's precritical (or premodern) view, only the mind that has been adequately tutored is capable of attaining clarity. Ironically, the Scriptures themselves were one of the means by which the mind was tutored.[21] For Calvin, Scripture is something to be looked *through* rather than *at*.[22] The scope of the gospel story is of such magnitude that it leaves no non-narrated place for us to stand to get a bird's-eye view of its veracity. For the master narrative of the Scriptures laces the Old and New Testaments together in a single story. This story not only affirms continuity between the Old and New Testament worlds, it also tells an eschatological tale. In other words, the plotline of this single story races underneath the reader's feet and off into a future whose final end is the reconciliation of creation with Creator under the reign of King Jesus. This is the story that has been embraced and embodied in Christian communities since their inception. As a consequence of the magnitude of the story's scope and the unbroken chain of its historical embodiments, it borders on the asinine for a lone reader to judge the truthfulness of the story by the meager criterion of his or her own untutored experience. On the contrary, argues Calvin, the scattered details of our lives are brought into focus by reading them through the lens of the story's setting, characters, plot, and ending. This reading strategy is what Calvin sees as the means of the Spirit's illumination.

In the end, despite Calvin's forensic style, his approach to Scripture may place him nearer to the medieval mystics than to analytic philosophers since Kant.[23] I only mean to point out that reading through the lens of Scripture requires a narrative reading strategy that was natural to Calvin but is foreign to us. And to the extent that postmodernism naturally eschews the hubris of analytic philosophy as well as the modernist myth of objectivity, it does well. Yet a postmodern reading strategy does not thereby turn a blind eye to historical-critical concerns. It mattered, for example, to the original recipients of John's Gospel that Thomas's attestation, "My Lord and my God!" (20:28 NRSV), was circulating during the reign of Domitian, to whom pagan crowds were forced to chant, *Dominus et Deus noster*—"Our lord and our god!"[24] And it matters that the very word for "peacemaker" that Jesus used to describe the children of God appeared on Roman coins as a tribute to Caesar as the "Son of God" who alone maintained the Pax Romana.[25] For once the historical context of Thomas's claim and Jesus' words is made clear, we are able to see that the loyalty to Jesus was a *political* loyalty to a radically new community that rivaled all other allegiances, especially allegiance to the state. Nevertheless, all such historical concerns are simply preamble to the critically important moment when readers come to see their own world in light of the biblical world. What ultimately effects this change of outlook is the power of Spirit-implemented narrative.[26]

First, stories have a way of setting the vocabulary and categories with which we see. I remember that when I was a kid one of my favorite brands of store-bought cookies was called "Yes!" cookies. The more I repeated the word *yes*, the weirder it sounded and the less obvious it was that it meant what it did. As Wittgenstein reminds us, we cannot fixate on a word to understand its meaning. Nor can we simply tell people they are sinners as if that term were self-evident. Secular persons' urgent need to learn the basic vocabulary of the gospel is what makes the "Bowl of Affliction" segment so powerful for participants of the Jesus Freakend. By role-playing the characters who fill the stories of the Gospels—the lame, the blind, the impoverished, the lepers—participants begin to get the picture that sin is not simply moral impurity. It is that and much, much worse. Think of the paralytic next to the pool of Bethesda (John 5:1–7). There he lies, so close to the very waters that could heal him, but those who are afflicted with lesser illnesses can move much faster than he can and invariably beat him into the water and are healed in his place. In a world of all-out competition, people don't take their turns in proper order when healing is at stake, and the par-

alytic loses every time. That is the powerlessness that sin pro-
duces. Or think of the grip that Pharisaic law had on the inhab-
itants of Palestine for whom healing was a breach of the Sab-
bath! Story after biblical story enriches our understanding of
sin as not merely impurity, but also bondage, powerlessness,
stain, disease, and poverty.

Second, stories shape the way we see because they are the
only means we have for identifying characters. If I talk about
Aristotle and you say, "Aristotle who?" I can only clarify who I
mean by recounting to Aristotle's story. "He was a famous, now
deceased, Greek." At this point you might be confused, for you
have in mind a twentieth-century aristocrat who married John F.
Kennedy's widow. The confusion ends only when I supply a summary of Aristotle's story that is rich enough to exclude all other
Aristotles: "famous, dead, Greek, student of Plato, teacher of
Alexander the Great." And of course, all these snippets are shorthand for episodes in the story of Aristotle's life. The same holds
true for the telling of the Christian story. When the nonbeliever
wonders "What kind of God? What kind of world? What kind of
people?" we say, "This kind" and proceed to tell stories. Stories
are not simply ornamental. They are the only way to settle who
we mean.

Third, stories cultivate our skill for seeing life in some ways
rather than others. One of the symptoms of our sinful condition
is our tendency to imagine that it is our responsibility to make
events turn out well. If we think it is our job to make history turn
out all right, then we imagine that the relationship between our
actions and the events around us is one of cause to effect. Consequently, we tend to measure our actions by the criterion of
effectiveness. As any church-growth handbook will show, even
those who serve others in ministry succumb to the ubiquitous
pressure to evaluate their strategies precisely in terms of their
effectiveness. This outlook is especially commonplace in our
technological society; any account of scientific advancement is
chiefly a tale of effective prediction, manipulation, and control
of the outcomes.

But there is an alternative way of viewing things. John
Howard Yoder suggests that the relationship between the actions
we take and eventual outcomes is one not of cause to effect but
of death to resurrection.[27] Instead of evaluating human actions

on the basis of their utility, we can regard our actions as deeds capable of embodying and reflecting the form of Jesus' story. We ought to measure our actions in terms of their faithfulness: do they faithfully reproduce the cruciform pattern of Jesus' life and death and resurrection?

The power of Jesus' resurrection was brought home to me when I was searching for a permanent teaching job. By the time I finished my doctoral work in spring of 1998, I had already been teaching as an adjunct faculty member for several years, all the while filing seemingly endless job applications. On the one hand, I grew ever more hopeful; each year I got more interviews. But on the other hand, I grew less hopeful, for there seemed to be no connection whatsoever between my activity and actually getting a job. Well-meaning friends told me that the most important thing was to "make those phone calls and keep my name out there." But academia doesn't play by the same rules as the business world. There is absolutely no way to coerce a committee to grant an interview. In fact, applications are welcomed only by schools that have previously commenced a search for a position for which funding is available. So a would-be candidate sends a letter of intent and a résumé in September. If fortunate, the applicant is granted an informal interview at a professional conference in November. Then more waiting for a call for an on-campus interview, which may or may not come, but the applicant will know for sure by May. And then, of course, the cycle is over for the year, and typically the would-be teacher must wait until the following September to try again.

"There must be *something* you can do," my friends would say. Nope. Nothing helps. Can you imagine professors being wowed by a candidate's snazzy clothes or expensive résumé paper? Granted, personal connections may prove handy. But if you don't have those, how can they be arranged? What about experience? Well, that's a catch-22. If you teach as an adjunct too long, prospective schools begin to treat you as damaged goods. But if you aren't teaching at all, you are deemed to be out of the field!

In the fall of 2000, just before Thanksgiving, I made my dutiful journey to attend yet another conference of the American Academy of Religion, this time in Nashville, Tennessee. About seven thousand professors in theology and religion of all sorts attend, so although networking is on my agenda, it is easy to get lost in the shuffle. This time I tried to chum around with faculty from one seminary in particular that I hoped would take an interest in me. (Unbeknownst to me, I was blackballed from the start because of my dissertation topic.) The most hopeful thing I had going was an informal thirty-minute interview I had landed with a private four-year university in the Midwest. I thought the interview went smashingly. However, they didn't. About a week later I got a letter saying that of the fourteen candidates they had interviewed, I was not in the top three. Ergo, I was not to be given further consideration.

I was devastated. In the previous three years I had applied to something like forty-eight schools, but I had only been interviewed a handful of times—usually on the telephone. I had lost out on positions because I was too conservative, because I was too liberal, because I had argued with committee members, because I had failed to argue with committee members, because I was too old, because I was too young, because I did not have enough teaching experience, because I had taught as an adjunct too long, and, in at least one instance, because I am male.

Although I had taught at seven institutions in five cities in two states and two countries, I couldn't suppress a sadness in my spirit and a profound temptation to doubt myself. But I found solace in the hope that God intended the pattern of my life to conform to the whole pattern of Jesus—to his life, death, and resurrection—not merely to his death. Although I could not engineer a happy outcome to my job search, it dawned on me that in trying to remain faithful to Jesus during the search, it was right for me to expect resurrection. I knew I could not predict in advance what resurrection would look like, but I wrote to a friend that it was fitting, on the basis of the story of Jesus' resurrection, for me to hope that in ten years I would be able to look back and say, "Hah! Resurrection!"

I recount my job search not because it has a happy ending (two candidates dropped out of the search at the Midwestern school, and I slid in as number five and won the day), but to describe the way the story of Jesus shaped my expectations long before the outcome was certain. Of course, not just any story would have served so well. But it is important that it was a story, not a doctrinal theory, that helped me to see my job search in the right way.

The reading strategy that Calvin employed (as did fifteen centuries of believers before him) is a tribute to the wisdom of God in sending us redemption by way of a story rather than a formula, theory, or doctrine. It is that power of narrative that participants of the Jesus Freakend tap into. As they reenact episodes from the biblical master story, the story itself gets a firmer grip on their hearts and imaginations. Moreover, the participants make enormous strides in their ability to imitate. For living in imitation of Christ does not mean wandering barefoot around Palestine. Rather, it involves seeing the similarity between Jesus' death and Stephen's martyrdom so that we too will forgive our enemies in the face of death.

This is why Journey 2 is so poignant for its participants. When Kierkegaard said that truth is subjectivity, his point was not to deny a privileged place for truths that we recognize as objective. Rather, his complaint was that our fascination with objective truths can sometimes obscure the more urgent issue of how we stand toward such truths.[28] For example, we moderns become uneasy when we read that Jesus publicly humiliated his opponents (e.g., Luke 13:15–17), so we search for some way to explain his apparent intolerance and political incorrectness. We are relieved to discover that Ancient Near Eastern cultures were based on a system of honor and shame. As Bruce Malina explains,

> Now in the first-century Mediterranean world, every social interaction that takes place outside one's family or outside one's circle of friends is perceived as a challenge to honor, a mutual attempt to acquire honor from one's social equal. Thus gift-giving, invitations to dinner, debates over issues of law, buying and selling, arranging marriages, arranging what we might call cooperative ventures for farming, fishing, mutual help, and the like—all these sorts of interaction take place according to the patterns of honor called challenge-response.[29]

Thus, we reason, the Palestinian culture made it necessary for Jesus to outshame his opponents in order to preserve the honor that was rightfully his. Had he not won these encounters with his enemies, his public ministry would have been decimated. We breathe a sigh of relief. But notice what we've done. In fixating on this "solution" we have become enamored with the abrogation of the problem rather than allowing the text to interrogate us: Whose side am *I* on? In what ways is their shame *my* shame? Or for those who hear the Sermon on the Mount afresh during Journey 2, the terrifying questions may be: Am I poor? Am I meek? Am I persecuted? Why not?

Notice, too, that the reenactment of Journey 2 comes very close to what Calvin saw as the other primary means of Spirit-driven illumination: the sacraments. For Calvin, baptism and the Lord's Table do not simply commemorate Jesus' death and resurrection. Each time these episodes are reenacted, Jesus himself draws near to the heart of the faithful community.

The easy way that narrative serves as a powerful means of the Spirit's twin ministries of conviction and persuasion (John 16:8-15) may suggest postmodern adjustments we could make to modern modes of evangelism. One of the most widely used tools for evangelism is the mustard-colored booklet titled, "Have You Heard of the Four Spiritual Laws?" Some will claim that the tool works because a story can be boiled down to its essence and expressed in terms of universal principles or laws. This thoroughly modern misunderstanding of how language works cannot help but produce despair among kingdom workers when presentations of the four laws appear to be losing effectiveness as they fall on the ears of a culture that has grown increasingly deaf to biblical propositions. Would-be soul winners sometimes react by redoubling their efforts, hoping to offset the lower response rate with a higher contact rate. If they are successful, the underlying problem of spiritual deafness may be masked. Sometimes the workers become complacent, regretfully attributing the fruitfulness of former years to an irretrievable youthful idealism. Ultimately, they may quit the practice of evangelism altogether.

When faced with a culture that seems no longer able to hear the gospel, some try unsuccessfully to pare the Good News down to its bare bones. But it is the meat, not the bones, that is nourishing! This paring strategy may stem from a misunderstanding of the law metaphor and may be corrected by attending to the way scientific laws are used to improve the understanding of novice scientists who are en route to becoming expert researchers.

The "laws" of the Four Spiritual Laws are provisional speech-acts, or "law-sketches," rather than universally accessible principles. When philosopher of science Thomas Kuhn used the term *law-sketch*, he had in mind scientific equations such as "f = ma." To those who can read the code, the fact that force is the product of mass and acceleration seems obvious. But what force? What mass? What acceleration? Does the force of love equal the mass of the elephant times the acceleration of inflation? The ridiculousness of this last statement exposes the fact that one must be schooled in a certain way to recognize which force, which mass, which acceleration are relevant. How do we come to recognize these? As any physics student can testify, the secret is story problems—tens, hundreds, thousands of story problems. The problems begin with simple apple-counting stories but lead the student toward complicated calculations involving torsion pendulums or the mass of protons. For each story problem in a series, an answer has already been calculated by an expert. These stories are deliberately used to hone the student's ability to recognize relevant details and put them together in ways that generate correct solutions. Eventually the (now graduate) student joins the ranks at the leading edge of research, where the data are ambiguous and no one is completely sure what solution will make the best sense.

A rich history of shared know-how is encapsulated in the law-sketch "f = ma." The same can be said for the Four Spiritual Laws. Just as "f = ma" is not self-evident to kindergartners, neither is "God loves you and offers a wonderful plan for your life" necessarily self-evident to the unchurched. But if the Four Spiritual Laws are law-sketches, then we know where to look to unleash their power. We must employ stories that are rich enough to bring people up to speed with the shorthand version.

We can use the first spiritual law as an example. There are a number of trouble spots for the secular reader who encounters "Law One: God loves you and offers a wonderful plan for your life." As Kierkegaard pointed out, persons who occupy rival stages along life's way will be predisposed to hear words like *wonderful* in incommensurable ways. One hears *wonderful* in terms of hedonistic pleasure, another hears it in terms of societal benefit, and yet another in terms of saintliness. The word *plan* is also ambiguous. Is *plan* akin to an electronic schematic,

which can endure no variation, or to a battle plan, which is by
nature highly fluid and dependent upon the creative reflexes and
spontaneous adaptations of its practitioners in order to succeed?
Problems of similar magnitude haunt the modern notions of
selfhood presupposed by the words *love* and *you*.

Perhaps the most troublesome word for the secular hearer is
God. Of course, the word has been nearly evacuated of any theological content by the frequency with which it appears as an exple-
tive in casual conversations. Moreover, neopagan ideas of god,
rushing to fill the vacuum left in the wake of modern atheism, are
often nurtured by contemporary forms of amusement. Recently,
a computer game called "Black & White" hit the market.

> In the game, players assume the role of a deity trying to curry
> belief from tiny villagers through miracles and the use of large
> virtual beasts. . . . Black & White . . . is only the latest in a series
> of virtual experiences putting players in the omniscient role of
> building and destroying whole chunks of land or controlling the
> fates of innocent lives. . . . But Black & White takes a slightly dif-
> ferent tack, focusing more on the cause-and-effect of being a god.
> Good and evil are not present as opposing forces, but as viable
> options—when used in the right balance—for creating belief. Dif-
> ferent actions will create a different world for your inhabitants.
> Kill indiscriminately, and you'll end up with a bleak wasteland
> of fearful followers. Shower your world with goodness, and you'll
> create a bright (but possibly boring) Utopia.[30]

In such a milieu, how are we to elevate the comprehension of
secular persons so they will understand whom we mean by *God?*
By using stories.

Names are not labels. They are summaries. When as a child
I pinned dead insects onto cardboard and labeled each speci-
men—"ant," "grasshopper," and so on—there was no confusion
as to the meaning of each name. But the name *God* is not a label
affixed to an entity knowable by some sensory experience.
Rather, *God* is a shorthand summary of a vast array of stories,
stories without which we would not know of God at all. That is
why the Old Testament uses so many names for God: each name
recalls the reader to an episode in the story of God. For those
sufficiently familiar with the story, *Lord Provider* (*YHWH Yireh*)
brings to mind Abraham's near sacrifice of Isaac on Mount

Moriah and the divine provision of a ram that was caught by its horns in a nearby thicket. The event inaugurated a new mode of relating to God, namely, faith. We might say that the name *Lord Provider* is just a mental hyperlink for the full-text version. It is this longer version that teaches us the intentions and scope of God's provision. Familiarity with these stories helps us to see who it is that loves us and in what ways that which he offers us is wonderful. This means that the evangelist must be prepared to give thick enough descriptions and adequate enough detail in summarizing the canonical identity narratives so the would-be convert can see—through the lens of the stories of Abraham, David, Moses, Jeremiah, and others—the very face of God.

These have been chapters of stories. For each story recounted, recent trends in postmodern thinking have been presented to help us see aspects of religious conversion that were often overlooked in the modern period.

Doreen's story teaches us that conversion is a timeful process of enculturation into community. Consequently, we ought neither to be impatient nor to rush to the punch line in evangelistic conversations. Larry's conversion shows the centrality of language acquisition for becoming a Christ-follower. Evangelists ought to think of themselves as language instructors, grammar coaches, or partners in a conversation conducted in the language we call "Christian."

Allen's account illustrates the persuasive power of participation in a form of community life marked by the distinctive practice of caring for the poor in Jesus' name. His story reminds us that evangelism is, at bottom, doing what Andrew did for Simon Peter—inviting people to come and see by firsthand engagement. Because such an invitation presupposes a community worth getting involved in, the evangelist's zeal must not be limited to simple proclamation of the message; it must be broadened to include a passion for increasing the health of the community into which would-be converts will be invited. As Heidi's story suggests, catechesis is one way to vitalize the community and shape the outlook of would-be converts.

Finally, the Jesus Freakend illustrates the Spirit-ordained power of narrative. Christians are people of the Book, but the Book God delights for us to open for others is neither a philosophical treatise nor a formal logical argument; it is a collection of stories. The evangelist who would assist the lost in timeful conversions that are marked by participation and fluency in the historical life, thought, and speech of the church would do well to remember that the Good News is, above all, the greatest *story* ever told.

6

Retrospect

On Growing Churches the Hard Way

Modernity may be over. I say "may be" because it is yet unclear whether the trend toward holism (discussed in chapters 1 and 2) will carry the day. In the meantime, we inhabit a very confusing world. Those whom we try to reach with the gospel of Jesus Christ will have one of two minds. Those educated prior to, say, 1970 see the world through modern eyes. Those educated after 1970 are likely to have embraced any number of postmodernisms. The plurality of the term (postmodernisms) is indicative of the shift from a uniform, shared vision of reality to a plurality of rival, even incommensurable, views. How are we to convey the universal truth claims of Jesus to an audience that instinctively rejects universal claims?

I have already made a number of suggestions. But my suggestions have nothing to do with current attempts to disprove

121

postmodern philosophy and restore modernism to a place of cultural prominence as prologue to convincing unbelievers that the gospel is true. After all, modernism has been no friend of Christianity. Moreover, I find virtually no evidence that New Testament evangelists converted people *away* from Stoicism (or Epicureanism or Platonism or any other "ism") *before* telling them of Jesus. I do find Paul arguing, but never in the same way twice. He was a Jew to Jews and a Greek to the Greeks, a bold philosopher in Athens, but the epitome of weakness and fear in Corinth. And I find New Testament writers borrowing from Hellenistic thought to communicate with Hellenistic culture, but in a way that transformed their borrowings almost beyond recognition. John and Paul both allude to the hierarchical order of the cosmos (an idea of which later Gnostics would be especially fond), but they turned this order inside out, depicting Jesus both at the top of the cosmological order—for he is Creator—and at the bottom—for he was crucified as a criminal. [1]

Most significantly, I see the New Testament believers embodying the gospel in their breathtaking form of community life.

> For the Christians are distinguished from other men neither by country, nor language, nor the customs which they observe. . . . But . . . they display to us their wonderful and confessedly striking method of life. . . . As citizens, they share in all things with others, and yet endure all things as if foreigners. . . . They marry, as do all; they beget children; but they do not needlessly destroy their offspring [lit. cast off fetuses]. They have a common table, but not a common bed. . . . They obey the prescribed laws, and at the same time surpass the laws by their lives. . . . They are evil spoken of, and yet are justified; they are reviled, and bless; they are insulted, and repay the insult with honor; they do good, yet are punished as evil-doers. When punished, they rejoice as if quickened into life; they are assailed by the Jews as foreigners, and are persecuted by the Greeks; yet those who hate them are unable to assign any reason for their hatred. [2]

When the gospel is thus incarnated, the church can truthfully be called the showcase and foundation of the truth (1 Tim 3:15).

As William James observed, "The philosophic climate of our time inevitably forces its own clothing on us." [3] Consequently, the outlook of our audience ought to suggest to us ways of contextualizing the practice of evangelism. It is not surprising that an audience schooled by modernism's reductionisms (see chapter 1) may continue to respond to the style of evangelism that imagines apologetics as mathematical and church growth as technological. But for a growing number of people, the tidiness of modernity may be not only repulsive but counterintuitive as well. The challenge that faces ministers in a postmodern age begins with the embrace of mystery.

Early in the nineteenth century, Charles Finney instituted what he called "new measures" for revival.[4] The pressure techniques he employed, such as the "anxious seat" and the calling of each sinner by his or her name, grew out of his conviction that effecting a revival was quasi-scientific, at least as much so as growing a crop of corn.[5] Ironically, agriculture has become increasingly technological. Scientists enrich the soil with synthetic fertilizers and develop new breeds of corn capable of bearing four ears per stalk rather than one. Yet the evolution of evangelism has not kept pace with other scientific enterprises. In fact, evangelists are inevitably thrown back onto the words of Jesus: "This is what the kingdom of God is like. A man scatters seed on the ground. Night and day, whether he sleeps or gets up, the seed sprouts and grows, though he does not know how" (Mark 4:26–27 NIV). The growth of the kingdom is always marked by mystery. If we lose sight of this mystery, we can easily fall prey to a wrongheaded mind-set that mistakes "technique" for "practice."[6]

In the first place, evangelism is much more like sailing than like proofreading. In order to proofread a document, one needs only to be armed with a dictionary and a manual of style. What will the words of the proofread document look like? Exactly like those in the reference books. Proofreading a document for spelling errors is a technique whose criteria and outcomes can be completely specified in advance. In the finished product, either the words are spelled correctly or they are not. But not so with sailing. Sailing is an activity that requires skilled judgment at every turn. While manuals have been published to teach people how to sail, the actual sailor must still fill in the blanks: *When* are the sails to be trimmed? *To what extent* are the sails to be trimmed? *Which* sails? For how long? The skilled

123

judgments required of sailors are not unlike those required of evangelists. How rich a summary of the gospel does so-and-so need to hear? To which activities ought this person be invited? How much Scripture is enough for today's conversation? What to do cannot be specified in advance. What is required is skilled judgment.[7]

Second, evangelism is more like questing than like archery. When it comes to archery, the goal of each shot is obvious. The archer sees clearly the bull's-eye before releasing the arrow. The archer may lack the strength, steadiness, and aim to hit the mark, but no archer ever picks up the bow and asks, "Now, just what is the point of this contraption?"

Not so for questing. The heroes in medieval literature embark on quests long before they show themselves to be heroic. Along the way they perform feats of daring that win them the very amulet or talisman or elixir needed to overcome the witch or dragon or curse they are to face around the next corner. But most noteworthy of medieval quests is the fact that questors rarely know precisely what they are seeking or how they are going to get there at the outset of the quest. What they are questing after only becomes clear after they have gained the skills necessary for them to recognize the object of their adventure.

So too with evangelism. Young, zealous soul winners notch their belts each time a stranger mutters the incantation known as the Sinner's Prayer. But has a conversion begun? Maybe. Is the conversion legitimate? Hard to tell yet. Is the conversion complete? Certainly not. Is the ambiguity of conversion the fault of novice evangelists who are unclear about what they are after? A thousand times no! For anything worth doing is worth doing badly—until one can do it better. And one can become a skillful evangelist only by beginning poorly, but beginning nonetheless. Only one who begins, albeit poorly, has the hope of improving.

Third, evangelism is more like acting kindly than like cobbling. The aim of cobbling is always distinct from the one doing the cobbling. Shoes are complete in and of themselves. And at the end of the workday, the cobbler goes home, whether to get drunk or to play Beethoven, it matters not, because the shoes stay on the rack in the shop. In contrast, practicing kindness is self-involving in ways that cobbling cannot be. When I treat my neighbor in a particularly kind way, this pattern of action is the goal of my kindness. Furthermore, I have more at stake in practicing kindness than the cobbler has in making shoes because my actions constitute my character. The same can be said for the evangelist. Evangelism is self-involving. To proclaim the message without living the life is to be a trifler rather than a practitioner. *Excellent* is not an adjective that applies to the presentation of the message in isolation of the messenger. The power and excellence of evangelism is in the living.

Finally, evangelism is more like medicine than like parallel parking. When my son first learned to parallel park, he triumphantly announced that he could park perfectly every time. "It's easy," he said. "All you do is back up until this lines up with that, then crank the wheel hard until that lines up with this, then straighten the wheel, and presto! I'm in!" Needless to say, I was impressed. I remember parallel parking as the bane of my driver's test. I wished my driving instructor had shown me the works-every-time trick that Danny's teacher had shown him!

But evangelism cannot be reduced to a works-every-time technique. It is more like the practice of medicine. I once read a medical column in a science magazine recounting a conversation that ensued after an intern asked the supervising physician to approve sutures he had neatly applied to the left forearm of a teenage girl who, she said, had cut herself while moving furniture. "This patient needs to see a specialist," the expert concluded, then questioned the intern: "Which specialist?" Frantically, the intern's mind reviewed notes and flowcharts he had memorized in med school. Hesitantly he offered, "An orthopedist?" The senior doctor turned to the girl and asked whether she was right- or left-handed. "Left," she said. "Will you roll up your right sleeve please?" Her right forearm was crisscrossed with numerous scars from previous suicide attempts. She didn't need an orthopedist; she needed a psychiatrist.

Any attempt to capture and quantify the insight of the expert practitioner would be like trying to put on paper what makes one smiling face ironic and another sardonic. No flowchart can be offered to medical students that circumvents the slow, painful development of diagnostic discernment that marks the experts.

A technological model of evangelism mistakenly seeks universal procedures that can guarantee authentic conversions. But evangelism, like medicine, is organic. No iron-clad universalizable principles can be formulated that circumvent the hard work of developing skilled judgment in the messy business of sojourning with the dying toward the land of the living. Occasionally, a pattern of action emerges that seems to suggest an underlying principle. But the application of principles never turns out to be straightforward and unproblematic. Principles can only be implemented by those who already have a practiced eye and a trained ear. Thus Aristotle's lament about the difficulty of living morally can aptly be applied to the troubles facing the would-be evangelist: "but to do this to the right person, to the right extent, at the right time, with the right aim, and in the right way, *that* is not for everyone, nor is it easy."[8]

My suggestions for doing evangelism in postmodernity, then, cannot be easily summarized because they require of us more than simply the straightforward application of a technique or two. The suggestions I have tried to detail in these pages beg for us to trade our fascination with propositions for a commitment to cultivating fluency; to augment our penchant for individualism with a zeal for forming communities capable of embodying the story of Jesus; and to surrender our hankering after coercive proofs in exchange for the fragile skill of seeing the cruciform pattern of Jesus' life, death, and resurrection.

I am confident that in twenty years we will not find our cultivation of fluency, pursuit of community, and training in pattern recognition (namely, to see the cruciform pattern of Jesus' life, death, and resurrection) to be cause for regret. But I grant that in the meantime, the approach to ministry I am advocating has a decidedly uncomfortable and ad hoc feel to it.[9]

I keenly remember my baptism by fire into the challenges (at the time, *terrors* would have been a better term!) of campus ministry. I was only barely a college grad myself. I still recall the day when all my eagerness drained into my socks: I had learned that the "sector" of the university (itself forty thousand strong) for which I was responsible housed over one thousand students. My ministry supervisor that year became one of my closest friends. Although I eventually graduated from his team to direct a team of my own at another university, he and I continued to meet at semiannual brainstorming sessions of all the campus ministry directors in our two-state area. Together we watched the "me generation" grow up and graduate. In their place was a new breed of college student that made us all unsure of how to proceed.

At one springtime meeting of the minds, we directors were feeling the sharp tension between our falling numbers (of contacts, conversations, converts, and recruits), the specificity of our calling to make disciples of all nations, and our obvious shortcomings. With a growing sense of helplessness, we brainstormed strategies and methods, principles and techniques, but no one produced the key that promised to unlock the door to evangelistic success.

In the midst of the confusion, my friend and mentor, by then a twenty-year veteran of student ministry, strode up to the chalkboard and summarized for us the sorry state of our student ministries, the seemingly insurmountable challenges we faced, and the ironclad obligation we had to get the message out. We inwardly winced at the edge in his question "What are we to do?" And then came his quiet and powerful answer: *"Whatever* it takes!"

Notes

Preface

1. For a very interesting study of how members of other cultures faithfully follow Jesus in orthodox yet culturally specific ways, see Priscilla Pope-Levison and John R. Levison, *Jesus in Global Contexts* (Louisville: Westminster/John Knox, 1992).

Chapter 1

1. Rodney Clapp, "The Sin of Winnie-the-Pooh," *Christianity Today* 36, no. 13 (1992): 29.

2. Nancey Murphy and James William McClendon Jr., "Distinguishing Modern and Postmodern Theologies," *Modern Theology* 5, no. 3 (1989): 191–214.

3. Stephen Toulmin, *Cosmopolis: The Hidden Agenda of Modernity* (Chicago: University of Chicago Press, 1990).

4. For a more technical explication see Nancey Murphy, "Philosophical Resources for Postmodern Conservative Theology," in *Anglo-American Postmodernity: Philosophical Perspectives on Science, Religion, and Ethics* (Boulder, Colo.: Westview Press, 1997), 113–30.

5. For more on the inherent unpredictability of human systems see Alasdair MacIntyre, *After Virtue: A Study in Moral Theory*, 2d ed. (Notre Dame, Ind.: University of Notre Dame Press, 1984), 93–106.

6. Arthur R. Peacocke, "Chance and Law in Irreversible Thermodynamics, Theoretical Biology, and Theology," in *Chaos and Complexity: Scientific Perspectives on Divine Action*, ed. Robert John Russell, Nancey Murphy, and Arthur R. Peacocke (Vatican City State & Berkeley, Calif.: Vatican Observatory and The

Center of Theology and the Natural Sciences, 1995), 135. For other examples of autopoiesis (self-organization) see Hermann Haken, *Synergetics—An Introduction: Non-Equilibrium Phase Transitions and Self-Organization in Physics, Chemistry, and Biology*, 2d enlarged ed. (Berlin: Springer-Verlag, 1978).

7. Carl Zimmer, "The Slime Alternative," *Discover* (September 1998), 87–88.

8. See Arthur R. Peacocke, *Creation and the World of Science* (Oxford: Oxford University Press, 1979).

9. Émile Durkheim, *Suicide: A Study in Sociology*, edited and with an introduction by George Simpson, translated by John A. Spaulding and George Simpson (Glencoe, Ill.: Free Press, 1951).

10. For example, see Josie Glausiusz, "The Chemistry of Obsession," *Discover* (June 1996), 36. For a more technical discussion see Jeffrey M. Schwartz, "Neuroanatomical Aspects of Cognitive-Behavioral Therapy Response in Obsessive-Compulsive Disorder," *British Journal of Psychiatry* 173, suppl. no. 35 (1998): 38–44.

11. In the New Testament we learn that one of the first-century Christians' nemeses was the Law. The Law was so central to Jewish existence that it is proper to say that it *constituted* the Jewish people. In other words, the Law was not simply a moral reference point, it was embodied in the pattern of their life together. The Jewish people had undertaken to make sure that the Law never again was "lost" (as it had been in the Exile, before its rediscovery during Josiah's reign; see 2 Chronicles 34:14–33) by tightly weaving it into their memory and, more significantly, into the pattern of their everyday lives. This moral and religious reform reached the peak of its fervor with the emergence of the Pharisees in the second century B.C. So rigorous were the reforms they instilled, that had all of the hard copies of the Law been destroyed, it might have been reconstructed simply by reading it off the communal life of the people. But herein is the rub: the well-intentioned practice of discussing and deciding how the Law applied in this or that specific case resulted in the creation of a tradition of interpretation that became enfolded into what was meant by "the Law." In other words, the Law was not synonymous with the Ten Commandments, but with the reformed pattern of Jewish living that embodied this history of interpretation. It was from *this* Law, on the New Testament view, that the Jews needed salvation.

To give it an even darker cast, this Law—this socially embodied set of rules and practices—can be thought of as having taken on a life of its own. Just as the racism of the parents reproduces itself in the children of a bigoted home, so the Law reproduced itself by becoming the inherited norms internalized by each successive generation as the means for judging rightness and wrongness. And, of course, if this Law was the standard for judging right and wrong, it became morally invisible and thus a form of bondage: no one thought to question the Law because the Law inevitably passed its own moral standard. But this Law no longer expressed God's intent to bless the Gentiles through Abraham. To redress the situation, neither Jesus nor Paul advocated the abolition of the Law per se, but rather preached a gospel of the kingdom, that is, a new form of social existence, patterned after the person of Christ, that would be the incarnation of God's intentions——literally, "the Body of Christ." To this end, it took an outsider—i.e., Jesus the Christ—to create one new corporate person out of two hostile and seemingly incommensurable groups known as the Jews and Gentiles (Eph. 2:15–16). This new social entity embodies the old commandments, but in a new way: the law of Christ (1 John 2:7–8).

12. For further reading on the identification of "principalities and powers" (Eph. 6:12) with degenerate social institutions and structures of power, see Walter Wink, *Unmasking the Powers: The Invisible Powers that Determine Human Existence* (Philadelphia: Fortress, 1986) and also *Naming the Powers: The Language of Power in the New Testament* (Philadelphia: Fortress, 1984); and P. T. O'Brien, "Principalities and Powers and Their Relationship to Structures," *Reformed Theological Review* 45, no. 1 (Jan.–Apr. 1981): 1–10.

13. E.g., 1 Cor. 12:12–13; Eph. 2:15, 21–22.

14. It gets even more complicated for philosophers of language; we cannot think about language without using the very language about which we are trying to think!

15. Ludwig Wittgenstein, *Philosophical Investigations*, ed. G. E. M. Anscombe and Rush Rhees, trans. G. E. M. Anscombe (New York: Macmillan, 1953), §30.

16. Ibid., §33.

17. Ibid., §244; see also §257.

18. The notion of training is central to Wittgenstein's views. See chapter 4 of my "Changing the Subject in Postmodernity: Narrative Ethics and Philosophical Therapy in the Works of Stanley Hauerwas and Ludwig Wittgenstein" (Ph. D. Dissertation, Fuller Theological Seminary, 1998).

19. Ludwig Wittgenstein, *Culture and Value*, ed. G. H. von Wright and Heikki Nyman, trans. Peter Winch (Oxford, U.K.: Basil Blackwell, 1980), 74e.

20. J. L. Austin, *How To Do Things with Words*, 2d ed., ed. J. O. Urmson and Marina Sbisà (Cambridge, Mass.: Harvard University Press, 1962, 1975).

21. J. R. Ravetz, "The Varieties of Scientific Experience," in *The Sciences and Theology in the Twentieth Century*, ed. A. R. Peacocke (Notre Dame, Ind.: University of Notre Dame Press, 1981), 200.

22. W. V. O. Quine, "Two Dogmas of Empiricism," *Philosophical Review* 60, no. 1 (1951): 39–40.

23. Quine himself viewed human knowledge as a monolithic totality. In recent years this has given way to a more "ethnocentric" view that communities may differ from each other by virtue of their respective webs of belief. On this latter view see Richard Rorty, *Objectivity, Relativism, and Truth: Philosophical Papers*, vol. 1 (Cambridge, U.K.: Cambridge University Press, 1991).

24. Nicholas Wolterstorff explains that a great many beliefs must be already in place for us to recognize some events as data while disregarding other events as irrelevant. See *Reason within the Bounds of Religion* (Grand Rapids: Eerdmans, 1984).

25. Thomas S. Kuhn, *The Structures of Scientific Revolution*, 2d enlarged ed. (Chicago: University of Chicago Press, 1970), 151–52.

26. Ibid., 158.

27. For an account that emphasizes the way a shift between incommensurable paradigms is nevertheless rational, see Alasdair MacIntyre, *Whose Justice? Which Rationality?* (Notre Dame, Ind.: University of Notre Dame Press, 1988), especially 349–69.

Chapter 2

1. I am using the term *conversion* to describe what systematic theologians used to call passive conversion. Systematicians sometimes distinguished between active conversion and passive conversion. The moment God creates new life in a person, the very next action God takes is the bringing to human consciousness the reality of that rebirth in the form of repentance and faith. This is active conversion. *Passive conversion*, then, describes rebirth from the human side, namely, the first conscious act of the sinner whereby he or she responds to God in repentance and faith. See Louis Berkhof, *Systematic Theology* (Grand Rapids: Eerdmans, 1941), 480–92.

2. One of the difficulties a paradigm shift entails is the question of what to call the new paradigm. In a time of turmoil in which it is unclear which version or which paradigm will emerge as victorious, there is a simultaneous battle over vocabulary. In recent years, the term *postmodern* has increasingly been identified with the French school of literary criticism called deconstructionism. In order to avoid this confusion, I prefer to use the term *postcritical* when describing recent trends in Anglo-American philosophy.

3. Ludwig Wittgenstein, *Remarks on the Philosophy of Psychology*, 2 vols., ed. G. H. von Wright and Heikki Nyman, trans. C. G. Luckhardt and M. A. E. Aue (Chicago: University of Chicago Press, 1980), 1:§339.

4. Alasdair MacIntyre, *After Virtue: A Study in Moral Theory*, 2d ed. (Notre Dame, Ind.: University of Notre Dame Press, 1984), 210.

5. See Hans Frei, *The Eclipse of Biblical Narrative: A Study in Eighteenth- and Nineteenth-Century Hermeneutics* (New Haven: Yale University Press, 1974).

6. St. Augustine, *The Confessions of St. Augustine*, translated and with an introduction and notes by John K. Ryan (Garden City, N.Y.: Doubleday, 1958).

7. Ibid., 2:4–8.

8. My analysis of Augustine's conversion is indebted to Stanley Hauerwas, with David Burrell, "From System to Story: An Alternative Pattern for Rationality in Ethics," in *Truthfulness and Tragedy* (Notre Dame, Ind.: University of Notre Dame Press, 1977), 15–39.

9. Hauerwas and Burrell, "From System to Story," 184.

10. St. Augustine, *Confessions*, 10:27.

11. Ibid., 1:1.

12. For a narrativist approach to the challenges Christians face in a pluralistic age, see my article "The Gospel Truth of Relativism," *The Scottish Journal of Theology* 53, no. 2 (2000): 177–211.

13. Because Whorf and Sapir have an overly simple way of construing the relation of language and world, few find their work persuasive today. However, what repairs their work and salvages some of their better insights is the paradigm shifting work of the Cambridge scholar Ludwig Wittgenstein. It is with Wittgenstein in mind that I borrow selectively from Whorf and Sapir.

14. Cited in *Twenty Questions: An Introduction to Philosophy*, ed. G. Lee Bowie, Meredith W. Michaels, and Robert C. Solomon (Orlando: Harcourt Brace Jovanovich, 1992), 274. Whorf's most important essays have been published as Benjamin L. Whorf, *Language, Thought, and Reality: Selected Writings of Ben-*

jamin Lee Whorf, edited and with an introduction by John B. Carroll (1956; reprint, Cambridge, Mass.: M.I.T. Press, 1997).

15. George A. Lindbeck, *The Nature of Doctrine* (Philadelphia: Westminster Press, 1984), 60–61.

16. Ibid., 37.

17. One might object that gaining fluency takes a long time—too long for it to be a prerequisite for religious conversion. Perhaps. However, that many instinctively perceive conversion as instantaneous may itself be the product of a worldview shaped by Newtonian physics. While I cannot explore this possibility here, I do wish to make the suggestion that we reconsider the more Hebraic notion of conversion expressed by the word *shūv*—literally, "a turning." This conversion-as-process was exemplified by the early church's practice of delaying baptism and first communion until the Easter after the convert had completed catechesis. So Augustine became a catechumen in 384 but wasn't baptized until Easter of 387. St. Hippolytus mentions catechesis of three years, but this appears to be the maximum length of instruction. See *The Apostolic Tradition of Hippolytus*, translated into English and with introduction and notes by Burton Scott Easton (Cambridge, U.K.: Cambridge University Press, 1934), 43, 87.

18. Ludwig Wittgenstein, *The Blue and Brown Books* (New York: Harper and Brothers, 1958), 24.

19. MacIntyre, *After Virtue*, 216.

20. Hans Frei, *Eclipse of Biblical Narrative*, 17–50.

21. St. Augustine, "To Jerome," in *Letters*, vol. 1 (1–82), ed. Roy Joseph Deferrari et al., trans. Sister Wilfrid Parsons, S.N.D., The Fathers of the Church (Washington, D.C.: The Catholic University of America Press, 1951), 392.

22. The word *canon* originally meant a measure or rule. When biblical texts function as canonical Scripture (rather than say, as literature), they embody the rule or pattern under which authority believers willingly submit themselves. I have found Nicholas Lash a helpful guide on these matters. See his "Easter Meaning," in *Theology on the Way to Emmaus* (London: SCM Press, 1986), 167–85.

23. St. Augustine, *Confessions*, 5.10–6.5.

24. John Calvin, *Institutes of the Christian Religion*, Library of Christian Classics, Ford Lewis Battles, series ed. (Philadelphia: Westminster Press, 1960), I.14.1.

Chapter 3

1. Lawrence Hinman writes that "what one is saying sets the limits of valid philosophical discourse. A philosophical style is wrong when it naively steps outside the limits which are being established by what is being said, i.e., when the presuppositions of a certain mode of speaking contradict what is being said" ("Philosophy and Style," *Monist* 63 [1980]: 523).

2. John Howard Yoder, "On Not Being Ashamed of the Gospel: Particularity, Pluralism, and Validation," *Faith and Philosophy* 9, no. 3 (July 1992): 285–300.

3. Alasdair MacIntyre, "The Fate of Theism," in *The Religious Significance of Atheism* (New York: Columbia University Press, 1969), 25–26.

4. Aristides, "The Apology of Aristides the Philosopher," in *The Ante-Nicene Fathers*, first series, original supplement to the American edition, vol. 10, ed. Allan Menzies (Grand Rapids: Eerdmans, 1965), 276–78.

5. George A. Lindbeck, *The Nature of Doctrine* (Philadelphia: Westminster Press, 1984), 129.

6. George A. Lindbeck, "The Church's Mission to a Postmodern Culture," in *Postmodern Theology: Christian Faith in a Pluralist World*, ed. Frederic B. Burnham (San Francisco: HarperCollins, 1989), 51–52.

7. Cited in Thomas C. Oden, *Life in the Spirit: Systematic Theology*, vol. 3 (San Francisco: HarperSanFrancisco, 1994), 218.

8. Cited in Alister E. McGrath, ed., *The Christian Theology Reader* (Cambridge, Mass.: Blackwell, 1995), 100.

9. I am using the term *consumerism* to connote what Ronald Beiner has identified as the distinctive way of life in liberal societies, namely, a way of life "characterized by the aspiration to increase and enhance the prerogatives of the individual; by maximal mobility in all directions, throughout every dimension of social life (in and out of particular communities, in and out of socioeconomic classes and so on); and by a tendency to turn all areas of life into matters of consumer preference; a way of life based on progress, growth, and technological dynamism" (Ronald Beiner, *What's the Matter with Liberalism?* [Berkeley: University of California Press, 1992], 22–23).

10. See Alasdair MacIntyre, *Whose Justice? Which Rationality?* especially pp. 349–69.

11. St. Clement, "The Letter of the Romans to the Corinthians (I Clement)," in *The Apostolic Fathers: Greek Texts and English Translations*, ed. and rev. by Michael W. Holmes (Grand Rapids: Baker, 1999), 89.

12. This phrase is Wittgenstein's: *On Certainty*, ed. G. E. M. Anscombe and G. H. von Wright, trans. Denis Paul and G. E. M. Anscombe (New York: Harper Torchbooks, 1969, 1972), §141.

Chapter 4

1. I do not think that any criteria can be supplied. What modes of ministry share under the rubric of postmodernism is at best a family resemblance.

2. As told by Brian McLaren of Cedar Ridge Community Church in the Baltimore–Washington, D.C. area.

3. This is called the *ordo salutis*, the order of salvation. One typical *ordo* comes from Louis Berkhof, who identifies seven logically distinct moments in salvation: calling, regeneration, conversion, faith, justification, sanctification, and perseverance. See Louis Berkhof, *Systematic Theology* (Grand Rapids: Eerdmans, 1941), 415–554.

4. St. Augustine, *Confessions*, 39.

5. St. Hippolytus, *The Apostolic Tradition of Hippolytus*, translated into English with an introduction and notes by Burton Scott Easton (Cambridge, U.K.: Cambridge University Press, 1934), 43, 87.

6. Gary Mar, "Evangelization Through Asian Eyes" (paper presented at the Logic of Evangelism [Society of Christian Philosophers], Concordia Theological Seminary, St. Louis, 1994).

7. Kim Hak Soo's *The Sermon on the Mount* can be viewed in Masao Takenaka and Ron O'Grady, *The Bible through Asian Eyes* (Auckland, New Zealand: Pace, 1991), 101.

8. Brad J. Kallenberg, "All Suffer the Affliction of the One: Metaphysical Holism and the Presence of the Spirit," *Christian Scholars Review* 31, no. 2 (winter 2001): 217–34. See also Nicholas Lash, *Theology on the Way to Emmaus* (London: SCM, 1986).

9. The "surprise" ending of Matthew 25: 31–46 should prevent us from being overly hasty in labeling which institutions are "Christian" and which are "secular." As is known, many so-called "Christian" groups lag far behind secular ones in social justice concerns. This is to our shame. The alternative is not much more comforting: as I read Matthew 25, I fear that the lagging groups are "Christian" in name only. I think many of us have yet to see in action the sort of authentic Christianity that Jesus envisioned and that the first- and second-century church lived out.

10. The construction of verse 56 employs an indicative verb to emphasize the factualness of "remains." This may indicate a causal relationship: one who "eats Christ's flesh" will be caused to "remain" or "abide." However, because a participle ("the eating and drinking one") is used for the subject, we cannot be sure that causation goes from eating to remaining. In other words, this text might be saying that the one who partakes in the Eucharist meal but fails to "remain" cannot be said to have eaten Christ's flesh. Whatever else one is doing, if one doesn't "remain," one cannot be said to be numbered among the eating and drinking ones.

11. Typically saving faith is described as being made up of intellectual (*notitia*), emotional (*assensus*), and volitional (*fiducia*) components. Each of these three is crucial; failure of any part means that faith is defective, hence possibly not salvific. See, for example, Berkhof, *Systematic Theology*, 493–509.

12. See, for example, Robert Paul Lightner, *Safe in the Arms of Jesus: God's Provision for the Death of Those Who Cannot Believe* (Grand Rapids: Kregel, 2000).

13. I will have more to say against propositionalism in chapter 5. Propositionalism has been challenged on many grounds. For a lively discussion see Telford Work, *Living and Active: Scripture in the Economy of Salvation* (Grand Rapids: Eerdmans, 2001). See also works by Terrence W. Tilley, such as *The Wisdom of Religious Commitment* (Washington, D.C.: Georgetown University Press, 1995).

14. For an account of the spiritual role that severely mentally handicapped may play in the lives of "normal" persons, see Henri J. M. Nouwen, *Adam, God's Beloved* (Maryknoll, N.Y.: Orbis Press, 1997).

15. For further study one would do well to consider Stanley Hauerwas, *Suffering Presence: Theological Reflections on Medicine, the Mentally Handicapped, and the Church* (Notre Dame, Ind.: University of Notre Dame Press, 1986).

16. As told by Doug Pagitt, pastor of Solomon's Porch, Minneapolis, Minn.

17. Thomas S. Kuhn, *Structure of Scientific Revolutions*, 62–64.

18. George A. Lindbeck, *The Nature of Doctrine* (Philadelphia, Pa.: Westminster Press, 1984), 37.

19. Richard Baxter, "Richard Baxter's Ministry at Kidderminster, 1647–60," in *Religion and Society in Early Modern England*, ed. David Cressy and Lori Anne Ferrell (London & New York: Routledge, 1996), 199–203. See also Richard Baxter, *The Reformed Pastor*, ed. Hugh Martin (Richmond, Va.: John Knox, 1956), 104, and J. M. Lloyd-Thomas, ed., *The Autobiography of Richard Baxter* (London: 1931), 76–84.

20. As told by Anthony Jones, minister to youth and young adults at Colonial Church of Edina, Minn.

21. St. Jerome, "Letter LIII, §§4–6," in *The Christian Theology Reader*, ed. Alister E. McGrath (Oxford, U.K. & Cambridge, Mass.: Blackwell, 1995), 49.

22. Michael Polanyi, *Personal Knowledge: Towards a Post-Critical Philosophy* (Chicago: University of Chicago Press, 1974), esp. 299–326.

23. Lindbeck, *Nature of Doctrine*, 62.

24. George A. Lindbeck, "The Church's Mission to a Postmodern Culture," in *Postmodern Theology: Christian Faith in a Pluralist World*, ed. Frederic B. Burnham (San Francisco: HarperCollins, 1989), 51–52.

Chapter 5

1. As told by Brad Cecil, pastor of "Axxess," a GenX congregation operating under the auspices of Pantego Bible Church, Arlington, Tex.

2. Berkhof, *Systematic Theology*, 503.

3. Ibid., 509.

4. For an argument that the Scriptures are clear only when read as a "privileged text in a privileged way within a privileged community," see James Callahan, *The Clarity of Scripture: History, Theology, and Contemporary Literary Studies* (Downers Grove, Ill.: InterVarsity Press, 2001). See also Stephen Fowl, *Engaging Scripture: A Model of Theological Interpretation* (Malden, Mass. & Oxford, U.K.: Blackwell, 2001).

5. Cited by Gabriel Fackre, "Reinhold Niebuhr," in *Reformed Theology*, ed. David F. Wells (Grand Rapids: Eerdmans, 1985), 264.

6. M. Polanyi, *The Tacit Dimension* (Gloucester, Mass.: Peter Smith, 1983).

7. This is what Alasdair MacIntyre calls learning a second first language by imagination. See MacIntyre, *Three Rival Versions of Moral Enquiry: Encyclopaedia, Genealogy, and Tradition* (Notre Dame, Ind.: University of Notre Dame Press, 1990).

8. Peter Winch, "Understanding a Primitive Society," in *Religion and Understanding*, ed. D. Z. Phillips (New York: Macmillan, 1967), 9–42.

9. It was not without irony that Westerners accused rain dancers of hypocrisy since they danced not in times of drought, but only when the rains were expected. But of course. They don't believe their dancing causes the rains to come. They dance to celebrate the coming of the rain.

10. On the connection between practices and authenticity see Nancey Murphy, "Using MacIntyre's Method in Christian Ethics," in *Virtues and Practices in the Christian Tradition: Christian Ethics after MacIntyre*, ed. Nancey Murphy,

Brad J. Kallenberg, and Mark Thiessen Nation (Valley Forge, Pa.: Trinity Press International, 1997), 30–44.

11. Bob Sabath, "The Bible and the Poor," in *Who Is My Neighbor? Economics as if Values Matter* (Washington, D.C.: Sojourners, 1994), 31.

12. I accompanied Bob when he went to turn himself in to the police. Ironically, the rumor of warrant for his arrest had been false; at least in the City of San Bernardino he had been skillful enough to avoid detection.

13. See Ian Thomas Ramsey, "Talking of God: Models Ancient and Modern," in *Christian Empiricism*, ed. Jeffrey H. Gill, Studies in Philosophy of Religion (London: Sheldon Press, 1974).

14. Cited in Terrence W. Tilley, *The Wisdom of Religious Commitment* (Washington, D.C.: Georgetown University Press, 1995), 23.

15. Cited in Stanley Hauerwas, *Unleashing the Scripture: Freeing the Bible from Captivity to America* (Nashville, Tenn.: Abingdon, 1993), 37.

16. As told by Mark Miller with New Song Church, Cleveland Heights, Oh.

17. Jerome, "Letter LIII,"49.

18. Calvin, *Institutes*, I.6.1.

19. Nancey Murphy, *Beyond Liberalism and Fundamentalism* (Philadelphia, Pa.: Trinity Press International, 1996), esp. ch. 1.

20. Immanuel Kant, cited by Stanley Hauerwas in "Some Theological Reflections on Gutiérrez's Use of 'Liberation' as a Theological Concept," *Modern Theology* 3, no. 1 (1986): 69.

21. Lest we think that Calvin was advocating an individualist approach to reading Scripture, we must keep in mind that the other "tutor" explicitly mentioned by Calvin was the sacramental life of the church. See *Institutes*, Book 4. See also Paul Chung, *Spirituality and Social Ethics in John Calvin: A Pneumatological Perspective* (Lanham, Md.: University Press of America, 2000).

22. Calvin's view of the role of Scripture in conversion is discussed in greater detail in chapter 2.

23. This is a relatively new field of exploration. See, for example, David E. Tamburello, *Union with Christ: John Calvin and the Mysticism of St. Bernard* (Louisville: Westminster/John Knox, 1994).

24. Raymond E. Brown, *The Gospel According to John (XIII-XXI)*, The Anchor Bible Series, ed. William Foxwell Albright and David Noel Freedman (New York: Doubleday, 1970), 1047.

25. Roland Bainton, *Christian Attitudes toward War and Peace: A Historical Survey and Critical Re-Evaluation* (New York and Nashville: Abingdon, 1960), 64.

26. See Brad J. Kallenberg, *Ethics as Grammar: Changing the Postmodern Subject* (Notre Dame, Ind.: University of Notre Dame Press, 2001), 49–82.

27. John Howard Yoder, *The Royal Priesthood: Essays Ecclesiological and Ecumenical* (Grand Rapids: Eerdmans, 1994).

28. See Søren Kierkegaard, *Concluding Unscientific Postscript*, with introduction and notes by Walter Lowrie, trans. David F. Swenson (Princeton: Princeton University Press, 1968), 116–224.

29. Bruce J. Malina, *The New Testament World: Insights from Cultural Anthropology* (Atlanta: John Knox, 1981), 32.

30. Omar L. Gallaga, "God Games," *Dayton Daily News* (Dayton, Oh.), August 19, 2001.

Chapter 6

1. "At the bottom of the ladder the Logos is said to have become flesh, to have lived among us as in a tent, a symbol of mortality, and to have suffered rejection by us creatures. At the top of the ladder, the Logos is claimed to be coeval with God, not merely the first of many emanations." John Howard Yoder, *The Priestly Kingdom* (Notre Dame, Ind.: University of Notre Dame Press, 1984), 51.

2. Mathetes (pseud.), "Epistle to Diognetus," in *The Ante-Nicene Fathers*, vol. 1: *The Apostolic Fathers—Justin Martyr—Irenaeus*, ed. Alexander Roberts and James Donaldson (Edinburgh and Grand Rapids: T & T Clark and Eerdmans, 1885), 26–27. Cf. 2 Cor. 4:11–12; 6:9–10; 10:3; Phil. 3:20.

3. William James, *The Varieties of Religious Experience*, The Modern Library Series (New York: Random House, 1902), 423.

4. John Dillenberger and Claude Welch, *Protestant Christianity Interpreted through Its Development*, 2d ed. (New York: Macmillan, 1988), 135.

5. George M. Marsden, "Evangelicals and the Scientific Culture: An Overview," in *Religion and Twentieth-Century American Intellectual Life*, ed. Michael J. Lacey, Woodrow Wilson Center Series (Cambridge, U.K.: Woodrow Wilson International Center for Scholars and Cambridge University Press, 1991), 28–29.

6. For a more complete account of the difference between practices and techniques, see chapter five of my *Ethics as Grammar: Changing the Postmodern Subject* (Notre Dame, Ind.: University of Notre Dame Press, 2001).

7. I had great difficulty thinking up an example of something that was a brute technique. When I check my children's homework for spelling errors, it requires no skill at all. The words are either spelled right or they are not. Ironically, my copyeditor for this book took exception to my example. She wrote "Actually, more skilled judgment is required than you might suspect, even just for spelling (what to do with variant spellings, treatment of religious terms that aren't in the publisher's style manual, diacritical marks in non-English names), and a lot more happens in proofreading than a spelling check." She suggested that I say something like: "For evangelism there is no style manual." I think Aristotle, from whom I get these contrasts, would approve. His point, after all, was that practical reasoning and skilled judgment is required in *every* facet of human life.

8. Aristotle, *Nicomachean Ethics* in *The Complete Works of Aristotle*, Jonathan Barnes, ed. (Princeton: Princeton University Press, 1984), 1109a: 28–29.

9. See William Werpehowski, "Ad Hoc Apologetics," *Journal of Religion* 66 (July 1986): 282–301.